REVISIONING

EVANGELICAL THEOLOGY

A Fresh

Agenda

for the

21st Century

STANLEY J. GRENZ

INTERVARSITY PRESS
DOWNERS GROVE, ILLINOIS, U.S.A.

InterVarsity Press® is the book-publishing division of InterVarsity Christian Fellowship®, a student movement active on campus at hundreds of universities, colleges and schools of nursing in the United States of America, and a member movement of the International Fellowship of Evangelical Students. For information about local and regional activities, write Public Relations Dept., InterVarsity Christian Fellowship, 6400 Schroeder Rd., P.O. Box 7895, Madison, WI 53707-7895.

ISBN 0-8308-1772-7

Printed in the United States of America

Library of Congress Cataloging-in-Publication Data

Grenz, Stanley, 1950-
　　Revisioning evangelical theology/Stanley J. Grenz.
　　　　p.　　cm.
　　Includes bibliographical references.
　　ISBN 0-8308-1772-7
　　1. Evangelicalism.　I. Title.
　BR1640.G74　1993
　230'.046—dc20　　　　　　　　　　　93-18090
　　　　　　　　　　　　　　　　　　　　CIP

17　16　15　14　13　12　11　10　9　8　7　6　5　4　3　2　1
06　05　04　03　02　01　00　99　98　97　96　95　94　93

To
Jim Hoover, Rodney Clapp, Dan Reid
in gratitude for their friendship
and interest in sparking a revisioning of theology
among evangelicals.

Preface

In 1989 I was invited to participate as a representative "northern evangelical" in a pastors' conference at the venerable Southern Baptist Theological Seminary in Louisville, Kentucky. The event was billed as a follow-up to an earlier dialogue between Southern Baptists and evangelicals. When I received the invitation, I found the very concept of such a dialogue fascinating. Until that point, the question of the evangelicalism of Southern Baptists had never crossed my mind. I had never entertained the thought that Southern Baptists could be anything but evangelicals. So this event forced me to realize for the first time that perhaps my sisters and brothers in the SBC, with whom I share a kindred spirit as "Baptists," might not also share with me the self-designation "evangelical."

More significantly, the invitation from Southern Seminary raised anew the question "What is an evangelical?" As I reflected on my assignment—namely, to speak to this issue—I realized that I could not approach the question with dispassionate and objective analysis. Rather, preparation for the event in Louisville forced me to enter again into the painful business of self-analysis, seeking to discover what it means for me to view myself not only in terms of my denominational heritage but also under the other label with which I had been raised: "evangelical."

From childhood I have always thought of myself as an evangelical. Even at a young age I looked on the organizations associated with the movement (which I only later learned were "parachurch") and the leaders of the movement (whom I only later discovered are not all members of my own denominational affiliation) as *my* organizations and *my* spiritual leaders. As I progressed into adolescence, I graduated from Child Evangelism Fellowship into Youth for Christ. In my college years I participated at one time or another in Campus Crusade for Christ, InterVarsity and the Navigators, with the Baptist Student Union thrown in for good measure because I was also a Baptist. In the context of the late 1960s all the parachurch organizations (except the BSU) joined forces on the campus of the University of Colorado under the banner of the World Christian Liberation Front.

In addition to my involvement in evangelical organizations, the great contemporary evangelical heroes were household words in the Baptist pastor's home in which I was raised. Quite automatically, therefore, I came to look to futurist Hal Lindsay *(The Late Great Planet Earth)*, apologist Josh McDowell *(Evidence That Demands a Verdict)* and evangelist Billy Graham as possessing the ultimate answers for inquisitive young minds. As I began to try my own intellectual wings and explore the rationality of the faith, the ranks of my heroes were augmented by Francis Schaeffer *(Escape from Reason)*, Paul Little *(Know Why You Believe)*, C. S. Lewis *(Mere Christianity)* and the theologians publishing in *Christianity Today*. Only later did the awareness fully dawn that these affinities had taken me beyond my denominational label and placed me in the middle of the then-mushrooming postfundamentalist evangelical movement.

My entire life, then, I have seen myself as a Baptist and as an evangelical. In fact, I have come to see that it is as a member of my denomination that I am an evangelical, and this because I participate in an evangelical denomination—the family of Baptists. And because I hold to a view of what it means to be and live as a Christian which is shared by a family of believers that transcends my denomination, I am able to see myself at the same time as a participant in that broader coalition called "evangelicalism."

In this book, therefore, I seek to speak as one who willingly and proudly bears the label "evangelical" and who gladly associates himself with the wider evangelical tradition within which the Baptist fellowships are best located. I affirm the classical evangelical worldview as *my* worldview. And I read the evangelical story as in a genuine sense *my* story—the story of my people.

As a committed Christian within the evangelical family, I am concerned for the future of the gospel witness in a rapidly changing world. The intent of this volume is to spark interest and discussion among thinkers who share with me the label "evangelical" as to how we should rethink key aspects of our theological agenda. Such rethinking—what I have called "revisioning"—needs to articulate the biblical, evangelical vision in a manner that both upholds the heritage we embrace and speaks to the setting in which we seek to live as God's people and share the good news of the salvation available in Jesus Christ our Lord.

A word of thanks is due to a team of people who were instrumental in bringing this book into being. The support staff at Carey Theological College are the unsung participants in my numerous writing projects. Specifically, I am indebted to the secretarial services of Lois Thompson and Beverley Norgren. And I owe thanks to my capable teaching assistant, Jane Rowland. I gained crucial insight and helpful suggestions for revising the manuscript from Professor Bruce Ware of Trinity Evangelical Divinity School and from my dear friend and "kindred spirit" Professor David Dockery, who is now the academic dean at the Southern Baptist Theological Seminary.

But above all, I express my gratitude to the editors at InterVarsity Press, especially Jim Hoover. I had approached IVP with a proposal for a one-volume systematic theology. Their wise counsel was to engage in this preliminary exploration first. Jim challenged me with the idea of writing a work that would call for some new paradigms and set an agenda for the future of evangelical theology. Whether I have fulfilled Jim's expectations and have indeed set a new agenda I leave to my readers to determine.

INTRODUCTION
EVANGELICALISM AND THE TRANSITION TO POSTMODERNITY

R ecently the executive minister of a North American evangelical denomination listed the concerns to be explored by the executive staff in preparation for the fall meeting of the think tank on faith, order and denominational identity. All the items on the memo focused on the task of being the people of God in the contemporary world.

The denominational leader's memo indicates that we live in the throes of an identity crisis. In recent years evangelicals have somewhat smugly pointed to the malaise that has engulfed mainline Protestant bodies and hierarchical traditions such as the Roman Catholic Church. But we are no longer immune from the grave changes transpiring in our world. The crisis is now infecting the coalition of theologically conservative and pietistically oriented groups to which we belong.

Evangelicalism is indeed in the midst of a crisis. During the last two decades evangelicals have gained unprecedented respectability. We have witnessed "the year of the evangelical," seen our people on the covers of leading newsmagazines and even found one of our own in the Oval Office. Yet we appear to be uncertain as to what constitutes being an evangelical.

In recent years, we have witnessed unprecedented growth in church membership. Evangelical congregations mushroom, while mainline denominations struggle. Yet there are signs of growing dissatisfaction with traditional evangelical ways of doing church.

Beginning in the final third of the twentieth century we have seen an explosion of evangelical scholarship. Evangelical presses flourish. Our colleagues read papers at professional societies. And evangelicalism is itself a subject for academic study. Yet uncertainty abounds as to the limits of evangelical inquiry. Nowhere is this seemingly unexplainable contradiction more evident than in the field that lies at the heart of evangelical self-awareness—systematic theology. An unrelenting spate of new theological treatises continues to pour forth from evangelicals seeking to capture the essence of the received doctrine. Yet we remain unsure as to what constitutes a truly evangelical theology.

The crisis within evangelicalism has led some observers such as Donald Dayton to conclude that the term *evangelical* may no longer be meaningful.[1] Can we therefore continue to speak of "the evangelical movement" or "evangelicalism"? And is there an evangelical theology that binds the coalition together, an articulation of the Christian faith that we who claim the evangelical label have to offer to the wider church, to the academy and to the world?

I am convinced that the current dissatisfaction affecting thinkers of all theological orientations, including evangelicals, is part of a larger cultural shift transpiring in the West. In fact, we may be in the midst of a transition rivaling the intellectual and social changes that marked the birth of modernity out of the decay of the Middle Ages. The world appears to be entering a new phase of history, often designated—for lack of a better term—*postmodernity*. The current disquiet within evangelicalism, therefore, heralds a challenge: we must prepare to meet the postmodern age.

Although it is not yet evident what will characterize the emerging post-modern era, several signposts are already visible. Fundamentally, postmodernism is an intellectual orientation that is critical of and seeks to move beyond the philosophical tenets of the Enlightenment, which lie at the foundation of the now dying modern mindset.

At the heart of the Enlightenment experiment is the authority of reason. Modernity seeks to bring the many aspects of reality under the scrutiny of human reason. This entails a claim to dispassionate knowledge, a person's ability to view reality not as a conditioned participant but as an unconditioned observer—to peer at the world from a vantage point outside the flux of history.[2] Further, modernity is optimistic. It assumes that knowledge, which it divides into separate disciplines, is inherently good. Modernity is spurred by a belief in inevitable progress. It assumes that science coupled with the power of education will free us from social bondage and our vulnerability to nature.

Whatever else it may prove to be, postmodernity is the questioning of these theses. Postmodern thinkers have given up the assumptions that reason has no limitations, that knowledge is inherently good and that we can solve all our problems. In response to the compartmentalization characteristic of the modern worldview, the watchword of postmodernity is *holism*— the desire to put back together what modernity has torn asunder.[3] But of greater significance for us is a related far-reaching change now transpiring. Postmodernism questions the radical individualism to which modernism gave birth and which has formed a hallmark of modern Western culture.

Modern North American society is indeed individualistic. The ethos of modern living elevates and celebrates the idea of the unencumbered individual, whose genesis lies in the myth of the autonomous self. Our inclination is to see ourselves as individual, self-determining subjects, as is noticeable in the common practice of defining ourselves primarily in terms of the choices we make. We suppose that as autonomous selves we exist independently of, and outside of, any tradition or community.[4]

More than we are willing to acknowledge, we evangelicals have bought into this modern thinking. Under the influence of the surrounding Western culture, we tend to understand the gospel in terms of the modernist focus on the individual. While it is true that the New Testament teaches us to proclaim the gospel to individuals, we tend to focus on the individual beyond what is biblically warranted. This has led to the crass individualization of the gospel and of the church that characterizes much contemporary church life.

There are signs, however, that the modern fascination with individualism is waning. Many thinkers are now calling for a more balanced understanding of the individual and social aspects of existence.[5] The current identity crisis in evangelicalism must be understood, at least in part, within the context of this broader cultural shift that is transpiring around us. The ferment within our ranks exhibits a deep-seated desire among contemporary believers for a new understanding of the relationship between the personal life of faith and the faith community. The disquiet within many evangelical churches is in effect a postmodern cry to the church to be the church.

The radical individualism characteristic of much evangelical thought and action is out of step not only with contemporary intellectual developments but also, and more importantly, with the vision found in the Bible and bequeathed to us by the forebears of our faith community. The transition to a postmodern age, therefore, demands that we rethink many unchallenged ideas concerning what constitutes the evangelical tradition and who we are to be as the contemporary expression of that tradition.

I believe that it is both possible and helpful to speak of a specific heritage called "evangelicalism." Our evangelical forebears sought to chart a new approach to the faith that would facilitate a rebirth of the biblical vision of God's design for his people. These godly thinkers were surely correct in their intent, and they have bequeathed the same challenge to us. We who view the story of evangelicalism as in some sense our own story must attempt in our day what they so nobly constructed in theirs. Not only should we continue to speak of evangelicalism as a distinct movement within Christianity, but it is also proper for us to speak of a distinctive evangelical theology, of a worldview that is derived unabashedly from the biblical message—the good news of God's action in Christ for our salvation—and that is faithful to the heritage of faith present throughout Christian history.

The transitional era in which we live demands that we give honest thought to how we ought to articulate in a new context the vision that inspired the giants of the evangelical tradition. In short, the transition to postmodernity demands nothing less than a rebirth of theological reflection among evangelicals, one that can lead to a renewal of our understanding of who we are as the people of God. To this end, we need to gain a renewed vision of evangelical theology; we must seek to determine what can serve as the foundation for a new vision of who we are as bearers of that grand heritage of the church we call "evangelical."

The following pages seek to contribute to the ongoing discussion concerning what theological method can assist us as evangelicals in the task of being the people of God in the contemporary context. To this end, the book moves through seven chapters.

Foundational to the whole is an attempt to delineate just what the designation *evangelical* means. Chapter one, therefore, raises the question of our evangelical identity, concluding with the thesis that to be "evangelical" means to participate in a community characterized by a shared narrative concerning a personal encounter with God told in terms of shared theological categories derived from the Bible. As evangelicals, therefore, we are a people of a unique spirituality—a unique vision of what it means to be Christian. Our vision—our evangelical spirituality—in turn both influences our theology and calls for theological reflection. This evangelical spirituality is the topic of chapter two.

As a people characterized by a unique vision of what it means to be the people of God in Christ, we share a common set of beliefs or a common theology. Interaction with what ought to lie at the foundation of that theology forms the central task of the book. Hence, my chief concern in this book is with theological method. The discussion of issues of methodology comes in four chapters.

In the first of these, I seek to set forth what ought to be the central task of evangelical theology. Chapter three presents theology as a practical discipline. It is the intellectual reflection on the faith we share as the believing community within a specific cultural context. But it has as its goal the application of our faith commitment to living as the people of God in our world.

The fulfillment of our theological task requires the employment of resources or "norms." Consequently, in chapter four I set forth three norms or sources for theology. Our task moves from the biblical message, through the theological heritage of the church, to the thought-forms and issues of the cultural context in which we live. By employing these norms, we can develop a truly evangelical theology, one that is biblical, confessional and contemporary.

Chapter five raises the central evangelical concern: biblical authority. In so doing, it focuses our attention on the first of the three sources for our theology. At the heart of our evangelical commitment to biblical authority is the thesis that the Bible is authoritative because it is the product of and the vehicle for the working of the Holy Spirit. Because it is the Spirit's book, the authority of Scripture extends to every dimension of our lives as believers.

A discussion of the final issue of theological method comes in chapter six. Nearly every systematic theology employs one or more foundational categories or "integrative motifs" in terms of which it organizes its task of reflecting on the faith of the believing community. This chapter explores what categories form the motifs of a helpful evangelical theology. I conclude that as evangelical theologians we do well to move beyond the kingdom theology so prominent in the twentieth century, while retaining the basic thrust of that motif. In addition to the concept of the kingdom of God, we should explore the idea of "community," constructing a theology of community that is oriented toward the theme of the already and the not-yet.

With these responses to the methodological questions, a discussion of the church rounds out the book in chapter seven. Our attention naturally moves to ecclesiology in that the church is the proper context in which we engage in the theological discipline. Our work as systematic theologians arises from our presence among the people of God, and it is directed

primarily back toward the congregation of Christ. Because of the foundational role played by ecclesiology in our theological reflections, a work such
as this book, focusing as it does on theological method, cannot avoid giving
attention to this much-neglected doctrine. The doctrine of the church in
turn serves as an example of the application of the theological method
proposed in these pages.

To the seven topics chosen others could be added, of course. A host of
other matters are important to the development of an evangelical theology
for the contemporary situation. For example, the question of science and
the Bible remains crucial. Also important is the perennial and related issue
of faith and reason. In the contemporary climate of religious pluralism,
some evangelicals are engaging in a reevaluation of the centrality of Christ
for salvation. And finally, a revisioning of evangelical theology demands a
revisioning of evangelical ethics.

But despite the importance of these and other issues, they are not as
germane to the central theme of this book as are the topics chosen for
inclusion. The central burden of the following discussion is the specifically
systematic theology that should characterize theologians who stand within
the evangelical tradition. And this somewhat narrow concern dictates the
topics of the chapters of this work. Most crucial to charting the foundations
for a truly evangelical systematic theology, I believe, are the questions of
the fundamental evangelical identity that motivates our theology and the
matters relating to the method that this theology should follow. I leave to
other thinkers or to other occasions the task and joy of exploring the other
important issues.

1
REVISIONING
EVANGELICAL
IDENTITY

The designation *evangelical* arises from the Greek term *euangelion*, rendered "gospel" in the English. Basically, therefore, an evangelical is—in the words of Richard Quebedeaux—"a person who is devoted to the good news that God has sent us a Savior and that we can be partakers of God's redemptive grace in Jesus Christ."[1]

The connection between the designation of the movement and *euangelion* has led many apologists to begin their descriptions of evangelicalism with an appeal to this biblical word.[2] The link between evangelicalism and interest in the gospel message is appropriate. Perhaps above all other developments within the church, evangelicals have stood at the forefront of evangelistic activity. For this reason, Billy Graham can declare, "Evangelicals may disagree on some minor points of doctrine or practice, but they unite in their common commitment to evangelism."[3]

Despite the special concern evangelicals have always shown for the gospel, this broad understanding is not exhaustive. Understood in terms of commitment to the gospel, *evangelical* would—or should—characterize every segment of the church and every Christian, regardless of theological loyalties, background or experiences.

If commitment to and possession of the gospel are not the hallmark of the evangelical movement, then who exactly are we as "evangelicals"?

The Historical Understanding of Evangelicalism

As evangelicalism has gained increased respectability within the broader culture, evangelical scholars have turned their attention to the task of defining what this label means.[4] Many observers of the movement describe it in terms of the history of theology.[5] Evangelicalism, according to this understanding, arose through a series of three historical waves or three concentric circles.[6]

The Reformation. The widest circle focuses on the sixteenth-century heritage. The churches that emerged from the German Reformation adopted the name *evangelisch* (evangelical) as a means of highlighting Luther's emphasis on the gospel and in order to set them apart from the Roman Catholic church. By virtue of this historical connection, all Protestant churches may claim the term *evangelical.*

Nevertheless, the self-conscious evangelical movement enjoys a special affinity to the sixteenth century. Adherents find the initial beginnings of the movement in the Reformation call to a return to biblical doctrine and its emphasis on personal salvation. Evangelicals often claim to be the sole true heirs of the Reformation, to have remained faithful to the gospel of the grace of God in Christ rediscovered in the Scriptures by Luther, Calvin and the other great Reformers.[7] Because of their sensed affinity to the Reformation, contemporary evangelicals would generally agree with Karl Barth's definition, even though not all would acknowledge the Swiss theologian as a bearer of that tradition: *evangelical* means "informed by the gospel of Jesus Christ, as heard afresh in the sixteenth-century Reformation by direct return to Holy Scripture."[8]

The Reformation heritage bequeathed to evangelicalism the great *solas: sola scriptura, solus Christus, sola gratia, sola fide.* As a result, the emphases on the authority of the Bible and the sole salvific work of Christ leading to salvation by grace through faith alone have characterized evangelicals wherever they have been found since the sixteenth century.

Puritanism and Pietism. More narrow than the Reformation circle is a second, which forms what Donald Dayton refers to as "classical evangelicalism."[9] In this second sense the term designates the particular expression of Protestant Christianity that developed from English Puritanism and Continental Lutheran Pietism. This wave of evangelicalism found its most distinctive expression in revivalist America in the eighteenth and nineteenth centuries.

No less than the Reformation, this second phase was significant in shaping evangelicalism. Puritanism bequeathed to it the quest for certainty of personal election and the vision of building a truly Christian nation. Pietism (and later English Methodism) fostered a desire for vibrant personal religion coupled with a social consciousness in the midst of the dead orthodoxy of the state churches. Revivalism, occurring as it did in the context of the Puritan concern for certainty of election, pressed an emphasis on an individually experienced conversion in the still-fluid developing evangelical movement.

In addition to the necessity of holding forth the heritage of Reformation doctrine, therefore, evangelical theology is oriented around the practical task of reflecting on and delineating the nature of the conversion experience, which as evangelicals we all share. This gives added importance to issues related to the interplay of the divine and the human in conversion, the marks of salvation, the relationship of conversion to sanctification, and the certainty of a believer's saved status.

Because of these roots, the genius of classical evangelicalism is its concern for or emphasis on a conscious experience of the grace of God in conversion.[10] Hence it is characterized by what Dayton calls "convertive piety."[11]

Convertive piety found its most fertile soil in the United States. The beginnings of American evangelicalism lay in the Great Awakening of the colonial era, a revival of such significance that it has been termed a "national conversion." This event left a lasting legacy on evangelicalism in the form of an emphasis on "experimental religion," a vision of being Christian that emphasizes that religious affiliation must be experienced in life.

The actual heyday of the movement, however, came in the next century, as evangelicals formed the religious establishment and even the national ethos of the United States. Historian William McLaughlin concludes, "The story of American Evangelicalism is the story of America itself in the years 1800 to 1900."[12] As the dominant religious force in the nation, evangelicals set out to fulfill the dream of the Puritan colonists and make the United States into the "city on a hill" they believed God had predestined it to become.

Nineteenth-century American revivalist evangelicalism was marked by a specific model of the church that arose out of the unique religious reality posed by the nation. From its inception, no single church group was able to dominate the religious life of the entire land. The new situation called for an ingenious innovation in ecclesiology: denominationalism, the principle that the one body of Christ is "denominated" into the various ecclesiastical bodies and traditions. Hence the several Protestant churches viewed each other as coparticipants in the one church that lies beyond the separate visible organizations. As a corollary to this principle, voluntary societies, serving as agencies for the advancement of the various aspects of the church's mandate, mushroomed. By means of their involvement in these societies, Christians who belonged to separate—and separated— church traditions could join together in causes on behalf of the kingdom.

Postfundamentalist "card-carrying" evangelicalism. If the nineteenth century formed the era of American evangelicalism, the twentieth brought its collapse. The demise was due to several factors: the failure of the revivalists to capture the mind of the era,[13] the sociological disruption that followed the immigration of non-Protestant peoples and the intellectual ferment triggered by the evolutionary theories credited to Darwin.

These changes plunged the churches into a squabble known as the modernist-fundamentalist controversy. In a series of twelve tracts *(The Fundamentals: A Testimony of the Truth)*, conservative leaders distilled the points of controversy. The declaration of "essential" doctrines adopted in 1910 by the Presbyterian General Assembly—the inerrancy of the Bible; Christ's virgin birth, substitutionary atonement and bodily resurrection; and the authenticity of biblical miracles—formed the foundation for the various formulations of the "five fundamentals."[14] These functioned as the rallying position of the fundamentalist coalition.[15]

But when the controversies subsided, the heirs of nineteenth-century evangelicalism found themselves divested of the control of most major Protestant denominations, which had "defected" to "modernism." In response, many of the remnants of the older fundamentalist coalition retreated from theological engagement with the wider culture.

Following World War II, a new coalition, which thanks to Harold Ockenga came to be known as "the new evangelicalism,"[16] emerged out of fundamentalism. It began as a protest by several younger thinkers against the internal division, anti-intellectualism, departmentalization of life and social irrelevance of the older movement.[17] Important as well was the formation of a new transdenominational body, the National Association of Evangelicals, designed to assist in the revitalization of conservative Christianity in America and to rival the National Council of Churches. The emerging new evangelicalism drew together persons and groups representing diverse backgrounds and interests, many of whom had participated in the fundamentalist movement—conservatives formerly involved in the mainline denominations (especially the Presbyterians and the Northern Baptists), dispensationalists, and participants in the budding holiness and Pentecostal movements.[18]

In its narrowest sense, therefore, the circle of evangelicalism encompasses a specifically twentieth-century phenomenon, a movement of conservative Christians that grew out of the earlier fundamentalism. Thus defined, evangelicals are a group of believers who consciously seek to stand between liberalism and fundamentalism. Like their fundamentalist forebears, they are committed to the basic doctrines of Christian orthodoxy in the face of the challenge of theological liberalism, with its tendency to accommodate the gospel to the modern, Enlightenment mentality. But to a greater extent than their fundamentalist coreligionists, evangelicals are open to engagement with the world and to dialogue with other viewpoints.[19]

Its rootage in fundamentalism has also profoundly influenced evangelical theology. The fundamentalist doctrine of inspiration gave specific formulation to the emphasis on biblical authority that evangelicalism inherited from the Reformation, and it paved the way for the emphasis on inerrancy characteristic of many evangelical thinkers. The fundamentals likewise moved the focus of theological debate away from the question of personal salvation, which lay behind the *solas* of the Reformation response to Roman Catholicism. In its place fundamentalism substituted the more intellectually oriented discussion of naturalism versus supernaturalism, which lay at the genesis of the struggle with liberalism and came to the fore in fundamentalist christological formulations. And evangelical theology's acceptance of the fundamentals oriented it to questions of propositional truth, in contrast to the interest in a person's relationship with God that had been so characteristic of nineteenth-century theology.

While not denying the standard "concentric-circle" understanding of evangelicalism, certain contemporary "evangelical-watchers" move beyond the older theory with its focus on the history of theology. They augment the thesis that evangelicalism is a theological movement by seeking to depict it in sociological terms.

Historian George Marsden, for example, argues that the "card-carrying" evangelicals who make up the postfundamentalist coalition constitute a religious fellowship, a transdenominational community with complicated infrastructures or institutions, somewhat similar to a denomination but more informal. Crucial for membership in the evangelical movement understood in this manner is the question of where one primarily derives one's self-understanding. Evangelicalism encompasses a group of Christians who see themselves as part of an entity from which they gain their primary religious identity.[20] Adherents look to the movement, and not to their particular denomination, for this identity. They are evangelicals first and only afterward adherents of a denominational tradition.[21] Evangelicalism is, to use the words of Russell L. Staples, "an identity-conferring community." Participants in the movement are aware that they are evangelicals, "even though they may have crosscutting religious affiliations."[22]

The Essence of the New Evangelicalism

Whatever may be the ethos of the movement today, the original intent of "card-carrying" evangelicals was to correct the deficiencies they found so debilitating in the older conservative coalition. Initially they focused on several crucial areas:[23] the development of a new social ethic, the setting forth of an intellectually credible Christian apologetic, a bold thrust in evangelism, the founding of institutions promoting education and scholarship, and transdenominational cooperation based on a sensed underlying spiritual unity.

As the twentieth century moved through its third quarter, evangelicals appeared to be fulfilling their earlier agenda. Evangelical apologists were crisscrossing the nation, speaking to college and university students. Evangelistic crusades had become a prominent part of the landscape, and commitment to evangelism received standardized and explicit formulation through gatherings such as the widely hailed Lausanne conferences. Evangelical educational institutions were thriving, and evangelical thinkers gathered for meetings of various scholarly societies, such as the Evangelical Theological Society. And many sought to give expression to the social conscience they believed was integral to Christian faith. In these and many other endeavors, evangelicals were cooperating across denominational lines, giving evidence that they viewed each other as coparticipants in the one body of Christ.

With these initial objectives largely accomplished, questions concerning evangelical identity and the shared commitments that bind such a diverse coalition, which had always simmered beneath the surface, reemerged to demand the attention of evangelical thinkers. One explosive issue soon gained center stage, namely, the doctrine expressed in the first of the five fundamentals of the old coalition—biblical inerrancy.

During the heat of the ensuing discussion, certain "card-carrying" evangelical leaders sought to make adherence to their formulation of the doctrine normative for membership in the coalition, thereby defining the movement in terms of adherence to one specific article of a larger, generally acknowledged creedal statement. To be truly evangelical, they asserted, a believer must acknowledge that the Bible is inerrant in all that it affirms concerning any subject which it addresses. In 1976 the former editor of the flagship evangelical publication *Christianity Today,* Harold Lindsell, even flirted with disfranchisement of those who differed with him on this issue: "It is my conviction that a host of evangelicals who no longer hold to inerrancy are still relatively evangelical. I do not for one moment concede, however, that in a technical sense anyone can claim the evangelical badge once he has abandoned inerrancy."[24]

The tenacity of Lindsell's position is demonstrated by its ability to evoke a strong echo eight years later in what proved to be Francis Schaeffer's final exhortation to the movement: "Here then is the watershed of the evangelical world. We must say most lovingly but clearly: evangelicalism is not consistently evangelical unless there is a line drawn between those who take a full view of Scripture and those who do not."[25]

Lest there be any misunderstanding as to what he meant by "a full view of Scripture," Schaeffer added, "the Bible is without error not only when it speaks of values, the meaning system, and religious things, but it is also without error when it speaks of history and the cosmos."[26]

Although not all evangelicals have been willing to make adherence to inerrancy the litmus test for membership within the coalition, many agree that the essence of the movement is best described in theological terms. This tendency is evident in several recent "dialogues" between evangelical thinkers and their liberal opponents. For example, three of the five points of discussion between the noted British evangelical John Stott and liberal Anglican David L. Edwards are theological: biblical authority, the atonement and miracles.[27] More recently Clark Pinnock and Delwin Brown delineated the differences between evangelicalism and liberalism solely in theological terms: methodology plus the doctrines of God, humanity, Christ, salvation and Christian hope.[28]

A paradigm somewhat broader than the strict focus on theology lies in the writings of a prolific evangelical theologian with a Reformed heritage, Donald Bloesch. Bloesch remains committed to a theologically oriented understanding of evangelicalism. In the 1973 Eerdmans publication *The Evangelical Renaissance*, for example, he sets forth what he sees as the "hallmarks of evangelicalism": the sovereignty of God, the divine authority of Scripture, total depravity, Christ's substitutionary atonement, salvation by grace, salvation through faith alone, the primacy of proclamation, scriptural holiness, the spiritual mission of the church and the personal return of Christ.[29] These doctrines form the core of the expanded discussion in Bloesch's subsequent two-volume offering *Essentials of Evangelical Theology* (1978-79).[30]

In the larger work, however, Bloesch moves beyond a purely doctrinal description of the essence of evangelicalism. Instead he claims that the movement's genius lies in doctrine plus experience: "My contention is that to be evangelical means to hold to a definite doctrine as well as to participate in a special kind of experience."[31] As a result, he finds in modern evangelicalism a tension between Reformation theology and Pietism.[32] But in the end, Bloesch opts for the Reformers over the Pietists, settling for an emphasis on doctrine. In keeping with his Reformation roots, the evangelical thinker elevates above the others the doctrine of salvation by grace, which to him "is the heart and soul of evangelicalism."[33]

As helpful as such theological delineations of the essence of evangelicalism may be, the history of the movement carries a poignant lesson: any revisioning of evangelical theology must begin with a rethinking of the typical "card-carrying" evangelical understanding of the essence of the movement as a whole with its focus on certain theological commitments. Rather than being its only authentic contemporary expression, the new evangelicalism of the second half of the twentieth century constitutes but one dimension of the broader evangelical trajectory within the heritage of the one Christian church.

Without a doubt, card-carrying evangelical leaders, publications and institutions have influenced the ethos of contemporary conservative Christianity. Nevertheless, the coalition by no means exhausts the circle of "convertive piety." As the historical roots of the movement indicate, many conservative Christian denominations lie within the larger orbit of "classical evangelicalism," even though they lack formal ties to the contemporary new evangelical coalition. And today many Christians who share much in common with "card-carrying" evangelicals nevertheless stand apart from the coalition that developed in the twentieth century. They continue to find their religious identity in their confessional or denominational heritage, which they believe has validity and an ongoing contribution to offer to the church and the world. As important as the postfundamentalist coalition is, therefore, we simply cannot narrow the boundaries of the evangelical movement to participation in any constellation of paradenominational institutions. Evangelicalism spills over the boundaries of the new evangelical movement that emerged after World War II.

The acknowledgment that evangelicalism is a wider reality lends a cautionary note to any attempt to fix once for all the nature of the evangelical trajectory. It especially calls into question the tendency to describe the essence of evangelicalism merely in theological terms, or more specifically by appeal to one theological expression. Throughout their history, evangelicals have no doubt cherished certain common beliefs. But instead of elevating any theological system to canonical status, we must move beyond the "fixation with theology" that sociologist James Davison Hunter finds characteristic of Protestantism in general and especially of the evangelical coalition.[34]

Bloesch's characterization of the essence of the movement as doctrine plus experience is a step in the right direction. However, I would assert that we ought to place the two dimensions in the reverse order.

Evangelicalism as a Vision of the Faith

The primary statement to be made about evangelicalism cannot focus on doctrinal formulations. Rather, "evangelical" refers first of all to a specific vision of what it means to be Christian. This vision is, of course, connected to a set of shared convictions. But it is not exhausted by them.

Because evangelicalism is not primarily constituted by a body of beliefs, the evangelical ethos is more readily "sensed" than described theologically. The "sensed" nature of the evangelical ethos is especially evident when we move out of academia and into the world of the evangelical people as a whole. As participants in the wider evangelical movement, we may not all be able to define exactly what theological beliefs constitute us as "evangelical," but we sense it when we find ourselves in an evangelical atmosphere. For participants in the movement as a whole, being an evangelical means sharing a sense of belonging, a sense that "these are my people." And this sense of belonging arises because as evangelicals we all are seeking to live out a similar, specific vision of what it means to be Christian.

The evangelical vision is present despite—or perhaps better stated, in the midst of—differences and diversity. It transcends racial and ethnic differences; it overcomes diverse sociological and social backgrounds. And it crosses political and language barriers. The common vision may be expressed through diverse worship forms. And it may be found in church buildings of differing types and styles—from the house church to the cathedral.

But what is this common evangelical vision? Fundamentally, I believe, the evangelical understanding of what it means to be Christian focuses on a distinctive spirituality. The evangelical spirituality is the topic of chapter two. Needed at this juncture, therefore, are merely some preliminary summary remarks which in turn move us toward the evangelical ethos that underlies this characteristic spirituality.

Foundational to the evangelical vision of what it means to be Christian is our shared desire to make the Bible come alive in personal and community life. Regardless of squabbles over formulations of the doctrine of Scripture, we are a Bible-centered people. Our first instinct is to take the Scriptures at face value—that is, to accept the biblical stories as in some sense true as they are told.[35] But more important, we believe that the scriptural texts are intended for living in the present. Ultimately, our vision moves beyond scholarly debate concerning "myth" and "genre" and even the heated controversy concerning "inerrancy." Beyond such questions, evangelical people seek in the Scriptures answers for daily living.

Similarly, the evangelical vision entails a shared sense that personal faith is to be vibrant and central to life. When true to what we espouse, as evangelicals we seek to bring our commitment to Christ into every dimension of existence. All of life, we declare, must come under the lordship of Jesus. A specific evidence of this attitude is the evangelical emphasis on speaking about the Lord as a partner in the journey of life. Whether in the marketplace or among Christians, whether in the old practice of "testimony time" in the Sunday-evening service or in the more recent emphasis on small care groups, the essence is the same: we talk about our relationship with the Lord, the One who is an active participant in our lives.

The shared commitment to the Bible parallels a shared way of praying. Whereas mainline churches may "say prayers," as evangelicals we "join in a word of prayer," thereby typifying what David Parker calls a "strong bias against the invalid objectification of spiritual practice."[36] We believe that God actually does hear and respond to the petitions formulated by the faithful believer. Above all, God quickly responds to the humble sinner's cry for saving grace.

Bible reading plus prayer constitute a central dimension of evangelical living—our emphasis on personal devotions. During this daily "quiet time" the believer actually communes directly with the Lord, speaking to God and listening to God speak.

The evangelical vision is marked as well by a shared understanding of the church. Thomas Howard correctly pinpoints the essence of this dimension: "If Bible reading and prayer form the taproot of evangelical spirituality, then fellowship is the characteristic activity."[37] Although some evangelicals belong to ecclesiological traditions that understand the church as in some sense a dispenser of grace, generally we see our congregation foremost as a fellowship of believers. We come together in a variety of settings, but one expectation is always present: we anticipate an experience of fellowship—the enjoyment of a spiritual bond with each other.

A related mark of evangelicalism is the shared means we employ to express our praise to God and our experience of God, especially through music. Again as Howard notes, "It is difficult for nonevangelicals to appreciate the place occupied by hymn-singing among evangelicals."[38] Consequently, evangelicalism is present in a small group of Christians from different countries who meet in a Bulgarian hamlet and in the midst of their time together are drawn to sing simultaneously in the three languages represented among them that grand old evangelical hymn "How Great Thou Art."

"Evangelical," then, refers to a specific vision of what it means to be Christian—a specific way of being Christian. This vision includes a fervent desire to make the Bible alive in personal and community life, a sense that faith is to be vibrant and central to life, a way of praying, an understanding of the church as a fellowship of believers, and a desire to express our joy and praise through vehicles of worship and testimony. But with these elements we have not yet pierced to the foundation of the evangelical ethos.

Beneath the specific evangelical approach to being Christian lies our common understanding of ourselves in terms of a life narrative. Hence the evangelical vision focuses on shared stories.

As evangelicals we speak about our lives in a special manner. Each believer recites a unified narrative of his or her spiritual journey. The details of the individual stories differ, of course. But a shared basic format provides the structure for them all, and shared basic motifs are woven throughout the various accounts.

The narratives we recite employ categories by means of which we bring into an understandable whole the diverse strands of our personal lives. Central to each of our stories is a testimony to the reality of a personal, life-changing transformation. Hence we speak of "sin" and "grace," "alienation" and "reconciliation," "helplessness" and "divine power," "having been lost" but "now being saved." And each story narrates a dividing line between an old and a new life, a line the narrator crossed by means of a religious experience through which he or she encountered the God of the Bible revealed in Jesus of Nazareth.

The stories we tell reveal that as evangelicals we share a common religious experience. We have met God in Christ, we declare. For some, this encounter may have occurred in an instant, a moment of time marked by a radical conversion. For others, it may have been a longer process. Yet for all the encounter with God occurred in time; it was and is an experience with the living God.

It is in this context of making sense out of life by means of recounting the story of a transformative religious experience that the Bible and theological commitment find their importance. No experience occurs in a vacuum; no transformation comes to us apart from an interpretation facilitated by the concepts we bring to it. On the contrary, experience and interpretive concepts are reciprocally related. Our experience determines the interpretive concepts we employ to speak about it; at the same time, our concepts facilitate the experiences we have in life. So also in the religious experience that we as evangelicals narrate in our life stories. The encounter with God in Christ both is facilitated by and expresses itself in categories that are of a theological nature and that arise from the Bible.

Putting all this together, I would suggest that central to evangelicalism is a common vision of the faith that arises out of a common religious experience couched within a common interpretive framework consisting in theological beliefs we gain from the Scriptures. As evangelicals we are persons who sense that we have encountered the living God through the gospel message of Jesus Christ. We describe this encounter by means of a set of theological categories derived from the Bible. These categories which form the cradle for this experience, in turn, constitute the grid by which we now interpret all of life.

As a result of our shared encounter with God in Christ, therefore, evangelicals share a set of long-cherished theological beliefs concerning God, themselves and the world, and evangelicals uphold the Bible as the source of these beliefs. Evangelicalism, therefore, is characterized by a distinct theology. But the evangelical ethos is more than mere theology. At its heart is a shared experience cradled in a shared theology, which serves as the context for our ongoing life as believers.

Hence Donald Bloesch is correct in asserting:

Our confession is not simply an intellectual commitment but is born out of the agony and joy of a transforming experience, thus becoming an existential witness. We cannot inwardly know the truth of the gospel apart from the evangelical experience, but this experience always points beyond itself to the reconciling and redeeming work of God in Jesus Christ in the history attested to in Holy Scripture.[39]

But more than the theological outlook itself, I believe, the way of experiencing the Christian life which as evangelicals we all share—the experience of belonging to this group because of this shared orientation to life—lies at the center of the evangelical ethos. Our cherished theological commitments, in turn, are important insofar as they serve and facilitate this shared life-orientation—and precisely because they are intended to do so.

The common vision of the faith—this experience of being encountered by the living God understood by appeal to categories derived from the biblical drama of salvation—lies at the heart of what the evangelical party within the church throughout its history has sought to maintain. Ultimately, the ethos of evangelicalism in any generation and in any expression— whether that of the sixteenth century, the era of the Great Awakenings or the contemporary postfundamentalist coalition—is an experiential piety cradled in a theology.

Before attempting to decipher the theological agenda that this understanding of evangelicalism demands, we must first delineate in more detail the specifically evangelical spirituality that comes to expression in our movement.

2
REVISIONING
EVANGELICAL
SPIRITUALITY

As Lane Dennis rightly observes, "The hallmark of evangelicalism has been its emphasis upon the experience of personal salvation—individual commitment to Jesus Christ as personal Savior."[1] The genius of the movement, in other words, is a shared religious experience, which, I would add, is couched in a shared theological language.

This understanding of the nature of evangelicalism is showing signs of increased acceptance within the contemporary postfundamentalist coalition. In fact, a fundamental shift in self-consciousness may be under way, a move from a creed-based to a spirituality-based identity. Attendant to this change may be the pending passing of the dominance of the older neo-evangelical establishment, which Richard Quebedeaux describes as consisting of "rational Calvinist scholastics, committed to the total inerrancy of Scripture and the propositional revelation contained therein."[2]

But if the formerly prevalent understanding is being replaced by a focus on spirituality, what is the shape of the emerging evangelical self-identity? And what significance does the new emphasis on evangelical spirituality bode for a revisioned evangelical theology? Before turning to these questions, we must summarize the changes transpiring within the movement.

The Changing Evangelical Self-Identity

The generation that shaped the postfundamentalist neo-evangelicalism in the 1940s and 1950s viewed the movement largely as a creed-based coalition. Originally, this coalition was founded upon the importance of ideas, committed to theological dialogue and dedicated to defining and defending classical Christian orthodoxy in the face of the challenge of liberalism and neo-orthodoxy.[3] Consequently, our elder statesmen continue to define the genius of the coalition and the mark of participation in it largely in theological terms. Evangelicalism, they assert, is based on adherence to certain doctrinal positions.

The older evangelical leaders readily admit, of course, that right doctrine has its natural outworkings, especially in right inward piety and right outward conduct. Hence, in 1979 David L. McKenna, serving as the president of an evangelical college, could claim, "We work for reasonable faith, realistic grace, and responsible piety."[4] But in the past the emphasis in this endeavor lay clearly on the intellectual or doctrinal dimension.

In recent years, however, this older neo-evangelical self-consciousness with its clear focus on doctrine has begun to dissipate. Its replacement places far more emphasis on spirituality as lying at the heart of evangelicalism.[5] The reemergence of an emphasis on spirituality as the center of the movement arises out of a broader understanding of the essence of evangelicalism which has always been present within the movement but often has been overshadowed by the preoccupation with doctrine. Hence, in a recent catechistic guidebook designed to initiate new converts into the family of faith, William W. Wells cites three specific characteristics of those who belong to the movement: evangelical Christians affirm the Bible as authoritative; they appropriate God's forgiveness and enjoy a personal relationship with God through Christ; and they commit themselves to the pursuit of a holy life through the spiritual disciplines.[6] Although they remain committed to biblical authority, contemporary evangelicals are displaying a renewed interest in the latter two of these hallmarks, both of which focus on spirituality.[7]

The shift in focus toward spirituality as a hallmark of true evangelical Christianity is in keeping with the outlooks of the broader historical movement of which the postfundamentalist coalition is a part. This suggests that the current change in evangelical self-consciousness may mark a return to the wider circle that formed the evangelical heritage prior to the twentieth century. Two important participants in that wider circle are worthy of note in this context—Puritanism and Pietism.

Evangelical spirituality finds its genesis in part in Puritanism. This movement developed a new kind of piety in response to the anxieties produced by the Calvinist doctrine of election, which in Puritanism made the problem of assurance of salvation existentially central.[8] In contrast to medieval paradigms, Calvinism couched the question of personal salvation in terms of God's mysterious election. While this theology protected divine sovereignty, it offered no clear criteria whereby a believer could be assured of elect status. As helpful as they may be, in the end no sincerity of profession of faith, no degree of faithful attendance at the sacraments, no accumulation of outward evidences of sanctified living[9] could suffice as marks of election. But in the face of the uncertainties surrounding the Calvinism they embraced, the Puritans did devise one definitive mark of election: the inward experience of God's saving grace. The attendant emphasis on conversion that this move engendered led eventually—at least in devotional literature—to an emphasis on a subjective mark of salvation, the inner, conscious experience of the new birth. Assurance of elect status, therefore, became the product of a believer's ability to narrate a testimony to a personal conversion experience.

Puritan spirituality,[10] therefore, focused on the preparation of the heart to receive the Word of God whether preached by God's faithful servants or mediated through personal Bible study, the godly walk of the individual who is accountable to God, and diligence to overcome temptation throughout the Christian pilgrimage. The life of faith was nurtured by the hope of heaven and love for the Savior.

In addition to the return to the rootage of evangelicalism in Puritanism, the newer emphasis on spirituality marks a retrieval of the pietistic roots of the movement. Especially important in this regard was the intent of the early Pietists to reform life, not doctrine. Consequently, as John Weborg notes, the point of contact between classical Pietism and the contemporary evangelical movement lies in "pietism's call for new life, spiritual fruitfulness, and a sense of difference both from the lethargic life of the territorial churches and from the worldliness of the members."[11] Evangelicals are pietists in that they, following in the footsteps of their spiritual forebears, focus on the dynamism of the presence of Christ in the life of the believer.

We ought not think of the recent shift in evangelical self-consciousness as an isolated phenomenon, however. Instead, it is part of a larger trend occurring in the church as a whole. This larger situation has its immediate impetus in the immense changes that have developed over the last third of the twentieth century. Perhaps no change has been as far-reaching as the dissipation of the theologically inspired activism of the radical decade of the 1960s into the quietism of the more tranquil era that emerged in the 1980s. The shifting of attention within the mainstream churches away from theologies and programs that call for militant engagement in the world sparked a renewed interest in a crucial topic that had laid dormant during the turbulent decade of the 1960s: the quest for spirituality. Evangelicalism simply could not remain isolated from the shift away from activism or "doing" toward quietism or "being."

The broader move toward quietism has been paralleled by an interesting shift in priorities in seminaries and colleges, both mainline and evangelical. Riding the crest of the mood of the times, many schools now espouse spirituality and the spiritual formation of students as their highest institutional priority.

The movement from activism to spirituality in evangelical educational institutions was symbolized by a seemingly insignificant incident occurring in the mid-1980s in an average-sized Midwestern denominational seminary. By vote of the faculty, the "professor of historical theology" became the "professor of church history and Christian spirituality." This change in nomenclature was paralleled by an equally significant shift in the thrust of the incumbent's research and writing. His interest in the great social reformer Walter Rauschenbusch gave way to a quest for finding God in the solitude of a mountain retreat center.

The contemporary interest in spirituality, however, is no purely new phenomenon. It is found in all the major religious traditions. And because it enjoys an impeccable pedigree already in pre-Reformation Christianity, it predates the evangelical movement, strictly understood. Mention need only be given to such thinkers as Augustine or movements as diverse as the ancient hermitage and medieval mysticism.

Although the emphasis on spirituality predates the rise of evangelicalism, the broader evangelical tradition may proudly take its place among the varied attempts to foster spirituality. This quest was indeed a major interest of its spiritual forebears, from Luther (who searched for a gracious God) to Wesley (who launched a quest for perfect love for God, or holiness), even though the evangelical vision of spirituality has taken many forms and expressions.

Despite the broad diversity that finds shelter under the broader evangelical umbrella, a common thread runs through the whole. Just as there is a typically evangelical vision of the faith—an evangelical understanding of what it means to be Christian—so also there is a typically evangelical vision of spirituality, a specifically evangelical understanding of the way of going about the task of being Christian. The recent rediscovery of spirituality, although not new to the church, raises anew the defining question: What is spirituality? To this we must couple as our more immediate concern the specific question, What then characterizes the particularly *evangelical* spirituality?

Toward an Understanding of Evangelical Spirituality

As recent attempts to define it indicate, "spirituality" is a broad and elusive term. According to David Parker, it encompasses "the state and condition of a believer, as well as attitudes, beliefs and practices."[12] Gordon S. Wakefield, writing in the *Westminster Dictionary of Christian Theology,* declares that the term is used to "describe those attitudes, beliefs and practices which animate people's lives and help them to reach out towards super-sensible realities."[13] Similarly, in the *Evangelical Dictionary of Theology* James M. Houston defines the word as "the state of deep relationship to God."[14]

Perhaps a more adequate, albeit still general, definition comes from Robert Webber. He writes,

> Broadly speaking, spirituality may be defined as a life brought into conformity with Christ. It recognizes that Christ's work makes us a citizen of heaven; that here on earth we journey toward that destination; that our journey occurs in the context of our membership in the body of Christ; that by worship our spirituality is continually formed; and that our mission in the world is to proclaim the Christian vision by our lips and in our deeds.[15]

Spirituality, then, is the quest, under the direction of the Holy Spirit but with the cooperation of the believer, for holiness. It is the pursuit of the life lived to the glory of God, in union with Christ and out of obedience to the Holy Spirit.

The New Testament sets forth two broad directions of aspiration within the context of the spiritual pilgrimage.[16] The documents articulate both a call for a holy detachment from the world and an admonition for dedicated involvement in the world. On the one hand, Christians are challenged to walk the narrow road to the kingdom. Consequently, spirituality is inward and quietistic. It consists in the denial of self, a mystical union with Christ, an ascetic approach to life, nurtured by the heavenly vision. On the other hand, believers are commanded to live in the world and serve others. Spirituality, therefore, is outward and active. It requires compassion, mercy and a zealous desire for justice, guided by a vision of what the world could be like.

How does the spirituality of evangelicalism fit within these biblical impulses? A helpful context for this question can be derived from the distinction between church-type and sect-type ecclesiological groups devised by Ernst Troeltsch. In his monumental study *The Social Teachings of the Christian Churches,* Troeltsch wrote that three types of Christian thought—church, sect and mysticism—appear side by side and are variously interwoven throughout the centuries. Of the three, church and sect are most important, he notes, for they assume permanent institutional form. Troeltsch's has become the classic description of these two expressions of Christianity:

> The Church is an institution which has been endowed with grace and salvation as the result of the work of Redemption; it is able to receive the masses, and to adjust itself to the world, because, to a certain extent, it can afford to ignore the need for subjective holiness for the sake of the objective treasures of grace and of redemption.
>
> The sect is a voluntary society, composed of strict and definite Christian believers bound to each other by the fact that all have experienced "the new birth." These "believers" live apart from the world, are limited to small groups, emphasize the law instead of grace, and in varying degrees within their own circle set up the Christian order, based on love; all this is done in preparation for and expectation of the coming Kingdom of God.[17]

Troeltsch's contrast, although overstated and stylized, nevertheless cries out for a corresponding contrast between church-type and sect-type expressions of the quest for spirituality. Within certain limitations, such a categorization may be valid and helpful. Just as church-type and sect-type movements follow differing visions of Christianity, so also they set forth differing approaches to spirituality. Hence the conception of saintliness assumed by a traditional Roman Catholic, which forms the best example of the church-type ideal, is radically different from that found among the Hutterites, which might rank as the epitome of sectarianism. Traditional Roman Catholic spirituality focuses primarily on participation in the sacraments while living and serving in the world, whereas the Hutterite finds in the colony a refuge from the entrapments of the world.

In keeping with Paul's delineation in 1 Corinthians 2:14—3:3, evangelicals place high value on being "spiritually minded" as distinct from "carnal" persons. By combining the cross and Pentecost[18]—that is, by relying on the victory of Christ and the power of the indwelling Spirit—they seek to lead what Watchman Nee terms "the normal Christian life," a life of growing conformity to Christ characterized by obedience to the will of God.[19] Evangelicals, therefore, have always been interested in "the victorious life," with doing combat with the devil, the lower nature and the world, and by the power of the Holy Spirit defeating these foes of the human soul.[20]

Consequently, the evangelical vision lies somewhere between the two categories of Troeltsch, albeit having greater affinity with the sect-type. Evangelicals generally sense a closer kinship to the simple Christianity of the Hutterite than to the pomp and ceremony of St. Peter's Cathedral. Their spirituality displays certain sectarian features, including a distrust of institutional, liturgical Christianity, an emphasis on personal religious experience and individual choice, and the necessity of regeneration and a holy personal lifestyle.

Yet the obvious conclusion that sect-type spirituality encompasses the ethos of the evangelical vision is less than fully satisfying. As we have noted, the heritage of the movement lies in part within English Puritanism, with its ideal not only of a holy church but also of a holy commonwealth. Consequently, evangelicals hold certain features in common with the mainline denominations. Evangelical spirituality, therefore, is tugged by the desire to be true to a basically sectarian vision while not fully eschewing the lure of the liturgical churches. This pull in two directions places a tension within the heart of evangelical spirituality.

At its best, therefore, we might characterize the core of evangelical spirituality as the attempt—sometimes successful, sometimes thwarted—to maintain a delicate balance between, or hold in creative tension, two sets of seemingly opposite principles: the inward versus the outward and the individual versus the corporate dimensions of holiness.

Balancing the Inward and the Outward

The spirituality of evangelicals constitutes the attempt to hold in creative tension the inward and outward aspects of the Christian life. The spiritual believer balances piety with activity.

Lying on the one side of this tension is the primacy we afford to the inward over the outward dimension of religion.[21] A nonnegotiable principle of evangelicalism is that religion is a matter of the heart. Although articulated differently by different representatives of the tradition, of paramount concern to all is the status of the heart. Whether from the pulpit or in private conversation, we continually ask, albeit perhaps in differing ways, "Is your heart right?"

Building from the writings of our forebears, from Augustine to Jonathan Edwards, we view religion as a matter that goes beyond the intellectual component of the human person. Religion, we argue, encompasses the "affections," the inner core of one's being. Christianity is not merely intellectual assent to a set of doctrinal truths. As important as belief is, it is not enough. To be a Christian is more than merely reciting the Apostles' Creed in church, for faith must entail a personal commitment that becomes the ultimate focus of the believer's affections. Convictions must not only be lodged in one's head but also penetrate the whole person, so that they become near and dear to one's *heart*. In evangelical jargon, "We must go beyond mere head-religion to true heart-religion."

The proper heart affections of the believer include the personal desire to engage in the Christian life and to enjoy fellowship with the people of God. But above all, heart-religion entails a commitment to Jesus Christ. This commitment is more than knowledge of the historical activity of Jesus of Nazareth or mere acceptance of doctrines about the Christ. Rather, it includes a personal attachment to a risen and living Person, with whom the believer experiences "a personal relationship." This inner life, in turn, both constitutes and is foundational for spirituality.

Our understanding of the commitment of the believer to Christ includes a strong emotional element. As opposed to an emotionally detached discussion of the attributes of God, heart-piety is characterized by a felt love for the Master. As a result, as evangelicals we are generally more interested in believers' personal response to Jesus than in their ability to formulate or even memorize grand theological statements about him. This may be evidenced in evangelical ordination-council sessions, which often spend more time on the candidate's personal testimony, sense of call and pastoral style than on points of theology. For good evangelicals are those who are able to sing from the depth of their beings, "Oh, how I love Jesus."

Because spirituality is generated from within the individual, inner motivation is crucial. We believe that mere outward form does not constitute spirituality. The outward act without the inward vitality is only dead ritual. Historically, the special object of our polemic has been the liturgical acts performed week after week in the mainline churches, which our evangelical forebears considered deficient in genuine life.

For this reason, the evangelical alternative forms a stark contrast to the concern that gave rise to the medieval Roman Catholic debates about the exact point in the Mass at which a communicant must be present in order to have fulfilled the attendance requirement. (The theologians eventually concluded that the crucial moment was the ringing of the bell and the raising of the Host.) Such a question is foreign to the evangelical understanding of spirituality.

For us, the *sine qua non conditio* of personal spirituality is not outward adherence to ecclesiastical rites, for holiness involves proper inner motivation. Hence the true believer does not come to church under duress or in order to fulfill some externally imposed requirement. Rather, we long to be at the gathering because we are committed to the Lord and therefore to the body of believers—the fellowship—as well. We are inwardly motivated, rather than outwardly compelled, to attend church services. The convinced evangelical sings with meaning, "I'm so glad I'm a part of the family of God."

Related to the emphasis on heart-religion is another interest intrinsic to evangelical spirituality, the pietistic concern for experiential religion. Faith must be a matter of experience. It must transform life.

The genesis of this concern lies in Pietism's emphasis on the theology of the new birth derived from the Fourth Gospel. The pietistic impulse maintains that a personal *experience* is foundational to the Christian life. Conversion is the irreplaceable, nonnegotiable beginning point of the believer's walk with the Lord, which in turn is the pathway of spirituality. As a result of this central interest, we continually ask, "Are you born again? Have you experienced the transforming power of Christ?"

The new birth, however, is but the beginning of experiential religion. Conversion is to be followed by a personal spiritual "walk," which is to be characterized by growth in holiness. James Houston speaks for many evangelicals when he describes spirituality as "the outworking . . . of the grace of God in the soul of man, beginning with conversion to conclusion in death or Christ's second advent. It is marked by growth and maturity in a Christlike life."[22]

Consequently, we continually check up on each other and on ourselves. "Are you growing in the Lord? Are you walking with God? Are you developing a friendship with the Lord? Do find that your life is being changed?" Such questions become statements of mutual caring, once a person has joined the fold. As an expression of this ethos, we sing heartily, "What a friend we have in Jesus," and the chorus "Things are different now."

This emphasis on warm-hearted experiential religion makes us notorious spiritual-temperature takers. If true spirituality consists in a heart warm to God, then assessing the relative warmth of our hearts becomes an important spiritual exercise. And if one's heart can grow lukewarm, as happened to the church in Laodicea—a situation that can invoke the wrath of the Lord—then continually monitoring one's spiritual temperature is a crucial endeavor. "Keep your spiritual fervor," we continually admonish each other, for spirituality is a matter of the inward personal condition.

The emphasis on the inward, on the warm heart, so central to evangelical spirituality, forms a creative tension when balanced with a parallel emphasis on the outward dimension of the Christian life. Spirituality may be a matter of the heart. But the Christian life also means discipleship, and discipleship is outward. In fact, for true spirituality to emerge, inward commitment must be translated into outward action. Inner convictions must be made visible; they must show themselves through the way Christians live. In the typical evangelical jargonization of the faith, "We must walk our talk."

But we have a special understanding of the nature of the outward acts we are called to perform. We dare not see them as means to obtain God's favor. Rather, they derive their significance from our desire to follow in the footsteps of Jesus. The spiritual life is above all the imitation of Christ. Discipleship means seeking to follow the model set forth by Jesus himself, for true Christians will reflect in their lives the character of Jesus.

This understanding forms the context for our attitude toward the rites of the church. In general we eschew religious ritual. Not slavish adherence to rites, but doing what Jesus would do is our concept of true discipleship. Consequently, most evangelicals neither accept the sacramentalism of many mainline churches nor join the Quakers in completely eliminating the sacraments. We practice baptism and the Lord's Supper, but understand the significance of these rites in a guarded manner.

Historically, evangelicals either never were sacramentalists at all or tempered the blatant sacramentalism of the medieval church. They were inclined to see baptism and the Lord's Supper more as symbols of God's grace or part of a personal obedient response to Christ than as magical means that impart actual grace. Consequently, some contemporary evangelicals so eliminate any vestiges of sacramentalism that they deny that any grace whatsoever is mediated through the rites of the church.

In any case, as evangelicals we generally agree that baptism and the Lord's Supper are to be perpetuated not so much for their value as conduits facilitating the flow of grace from God to the communicant as because they remind the participant and the community of the grace of God received inwardly, or because they belong to the obedient response of the believer or the believing community to divine command. Simply stated, the sacraments are a significant means to express outwardly what is already inwardly true. They are indeed outward, visible signs of an inward, invisible grace.

Our emphasis on discipleship as the imitation of Christ also affects our understanding of church life. We emphasize daily walk, in contrast to mere

Sunday worship attendance, as integral to being an exemplary church member. James Houston reflects this outlook when he writes, "Christian worship is not primarily a matter of special practices but of life style."[23]

The emphasis on daily personal walk means that a central motivation for attendance at worship is the desire to be admonished toward a godly lifestyle. The typical evangelical sermon takes up the challenge to embody this concern. Although the specific topic may vary, the point the evangelical preacher makes each Sunday is the same: "If you are a believer, holy conduct must characterize your life not only Sunday morning but also Monday through Saturday. What is heard in the Sunday worship service must be translated into action throughout the week. If this is not the case, then your faith merely fades into a useless 'churchianity.' "

This dimension of evangelical churchmanship—the emphasis on daily walk—both arises from and determines our understanding of the nature of the church. In reaction against medieval Catholic ecclesiology, our forebears forsook the view that the church is the dispenser of the grace of God. A person does not come to the church to receive salvation. Rather, a believer—one who has saving grace—joins the Christian community in order to participate with the people of God in the mandate given to the church. Consequently, the church is the voluntary gathering of the redeemed who are united in allegiance to Christ and in mission to the world.

Evangelical spirituality, then, attempts to maintain a balance between the inward and outward dimensions of the Christian life. We seek to hold in creative tension the warm heart and the life lived in imitation of Christ. We give priority to the inward dimension as the wellspring of the outward, but we consider the inward dead if it does not lead to its proper outward expression in the life of discipleship. Hence we sing with gusto the old gospel song that combines the two dimensions: "Trust and obey, for there's no other way / to be happy in Jesus, but to trust and obey."

The Personal and the Corporate
Our spirituality is characterized by tension between the inward and the outward. It is characterized as well by another creative tension, the attempt

to balance the individual and the corporate.

Piety among evangelicals has tended to be highly individualistic. "Bible reading" means private Bible reading; "prayer" means private prayer; "salvation" means being saved as an individual; "being in Christ" means having a personal relationship with Jesus; "the empowerment of the Spirit" means being capable as an individual to act. As Daniel Stevick notes, "The Christian pilgrimage is made alone. God's salvation is individually directed. His help is in an individual companionship. The way is the lonely route of personal sanctification, personally attained. And the goal is a mansion built for one."[24]

This characterization is to some extent accurate. Yet at its best the evangelical approach to the life of faith emphasizes the individual believer not in isolation but within the corporate church fellowship, thereby balancing the two dimensions of the spiritual life.

Without a doubt, we understand the Christian life as an individual matter. Both conversion and subsequent growth in the faith are first and foremost the task of the individual. All believers must shoulder responsibility for their own spirituality, for each is individually responsible to become holy and Christlike.

This individual-oriented emphasis in the matter of spirituality goes hand in hand with the traditional Protestant principle of believer priesthood and especially its offshoot "individual competency," known in some circles as "soul liberty." The principle of individual competency asserts that each person is both spiritually responsible before God and capable under the impulse of the Holy Spirit to respond to God. The individual "soul," therefore, must be granted "liberty"—that is, freedom from external compulsion—in religious matters.

The principle of individual competency carries a crucial implication for spirituality. It means that no one can be brought into right relation with God by another person or by the church. No person can claim to be a Christian by appeal to the faith of parents, the performance of some rite, birth in a certain nation or even personal religious affiliation. To use a favorite evangelical cliché, "God has no grandchildren."

In contrast to what we perceive to be the teaching of the mainline churches, therefore, as evangelicals we adamantly assert that true Christianity is a matter of personal commitment. In the decision for or against accepting Christ, for example, each individual stands alone. Consequently, evangelists appeal to their audiences as individuals, rarely as a group. "The decision to decide for or against Christ is yours; no one can answer for you," the evangelical preacher or testimony-giver asserts. And no evangelistic crusade is complete without a least one rendition of "Just as I am without one plea. . . . Oh, Lamb of God, I come."

What is true concerning conversion is likewise true with respect to spiritual growth. Becoming Christlike is an individual matter.

Nowhere is the evangelical emphasis on the individual more evident than in our understanding of the church. According to evangelical ecclesiology, just as the church does not mediate grace and eternal life to its adherents, it cannot mediate spirituality. This view marks a radical shift in the relationship of soteriology and ecclesiology, for it exchanges the priority of the church for the priority of the believer. Rather than claiming that the church precedes and makes the adherent a Christian, evangelicals have a tendency to reverse the order. Converted individuals, who by virtue of their personal union with Christ have received from God eternal life, are the building blocks of the church. The church, consequently, is to some degree the product of the coming together of the saved, who join together in part for the purpose of fostering growth toward spirituality among themselves. Whatever else it may be, the church, therefore, is a voluntary association of individual believers.

Because spirituality is an individual matter, it requires personal diligence and the application of one's resources. We continually admonish each other to take charge of our lives and apply ourselves to the task of spiritual growth. As a result, we strongly emphasize the so-called spiritual disciplines. Growth in spirituality requires that each of us engage in daily Bible reading and prayer, understood in terms of the morning "quiet time," which, we argue, has the power to set the tone for the entire day. Important as well is witnessing to others (or "sharing one's faith"). Not to be ignored in the process is church attendance, for even this can be a discipline leading to growth.

What evangelical believer of long standing has not memorized that hymn which expresses in poetic form the core spiritual disciplines:

Take time to be holy,

speak oft with the Lord;

abide in him always,

and feed on his word.

Make friends with God's children;

help those who are weak;

forgetting in nothing

his promise to keep.

The fellowship dimension that this hymn captures in poetry Houston expresses in prose: "Godliness and spiritual friendship reinforce each other, as a horizontal and a vertical way respectively, to inspire and to embody the love of God in human hearts."[25]

The emphasis on spiritual disciplines as vehicles for personal growth is evident in our typical evangelical admonition to each other to apply ourselves in the enterprise. "Get on with the task; get your life in order by practicing the aids to growth and see if you do not mature spiritually," we exhort. In fact, if a believer comes to the point where he or she senses that stagnation has set in, evangelical counsel is to redouble one's efforts in the task of exercising the disciplines. "Check up on yourself," the evangelical spiritual counselor admonishes. "Have you been reading your Bible? Or have you been neglecting your devotional life?"

The appeal to the individual likewise runs through evangelical proclamation. We pitch our preaching to the individual listener, with the goal being personal response. We are known for our continued use of "altar calls," which vary from merely having persons in the congregation raise their hands to inviting them to come to the front as a sign of their response to the sermon. "I want each one of you to pause, reflect and then come forward or go to the prayer room," the evangelical preacher exhorts the congregation at the conclusion of the service. "Decide now for Christ;

respond to the gospel invitation."

We may use the same basic form to encourage response to the parallel call to redouble our efforts in the task of spiritual growth. Whether the hearer is an unbeliever or a backslider, the plea is the same: "Softly and tenderly Jesus is calling, / calling for you and for me. . . . / Come home, ye who are weary, come home." As a result, at the close of a service the foot of the platform may be populated by persons "accepting the Lord," others requesting baptism or church membership and still others "rededicating their lives."

Our evangelical emphasis on the individual is also noticeable in missions strategy. In the late patristic era, as Christianity moved into the barbaric regions beyond the Roman Empire, missionaries often targeted their message to prominent persons in the social order—the tribal chief and elders, for example, or the king. The baptism of the leaders, in turn, led to the baptism of those in their domain. As evangelicals we tend to fear that this tactic too readily leads to a forced, syncretistic and superficial Christianity among the populace, and thus a shallow spirituality. While not denying the important role played by tribal leaders, our preference is to direct the gospel to all persons, and to all as individuals. For we understand spirituality to be the task of the individual.

While adamantly upholding the importance of personal piety, evangelical spirituality balances the priority of the individual with a turn in the opposite direction, to a corresponding emphasis on the corporate dimension of the Christian life. Although primarily the task of the individual, spirituality is nevertheless a corporate project. No one can hope to live the Christian life or grow in Christlikeness in isolation; rather, each believer needs the resources of the group in order to gain spiritual maturity.

We sometimes express the importance of the corporate dimension by employing the well-known analogy of logs in the fireplace. A group of logs will burn nicely when kept together. But pull one log out of its place, and soon its fire dies out and the log becomes cold. So also in the Christian life: Christians who separate themselves from the community of faith run the risk of losing their spiritual fervor and growing cold. As they participate in the community of faith, however, believers support each other. In this way all maintain their ardor; together they remain spiritually alive and warm for the Lord.

In the evangelical outlook, therefore, the individual, although personally responsible for his or her own growth, remains dependent on the group. All believers need the encouragement and admonition that they receive from one another. As Houston explains, "Christian spirituality engenders fellowship, and the communion of saints deepens its character."[26]

Like other emphases of evangelical spirituality, this acknowledgment of a group dependency has ramifications for our understanding of the church. The local congregation is to be an encouraging, supporting, admonishing community. Further, each member of the fellowship is to join with the others, becoming personally involved in the corporate task. We are called together not only to worship but also to enter into each other's lives and thereby foster and participate in community life, which is the essence of the ethos of the local congregation.

The principle that individual believers need the resources of the group results in a corresponding and typically evangelical emphasis on church attendance. We ought to be present for corporate church events. But the purpose lying behind this emphasis differs from that of liturgical churches. We do not tend to view attendance at church functions as a means of grace. Instead of an automatic channel of grace, the gathered community is a vehicle of instruction and encouragement.

This understanding, in turn, affects what we regard as the central element of the corporate gathering. Whereas Roman Catholics emphasize the Eucharist, in evangelical church life the focus of the worship service is preaching. Above all, we come to hear the sermon, which we view as the primary vehicle for the encounter of the individual with the divine. We listen to the sermon with the expectation of hearing "the word of God." And through this spoken word, God speaks to us as individuals. As a result, we find admonition, encouragement and even direction for life through our presence at worship. We gather to listen to the word, so that we can scatter to be the people of God in the world.

In recent years, however, evangelicals have begun to recapture a deeper sense of the importance of corporate worship both as an element in and as a focus alongside of preaching. One leader in this renaissance, Robert Webber, explains:

> Worship is the rehearsal of our relationship to God. It is at that point through the preaching of the Word and through the administration of the sacrament, that God makes himself uniquely present in the body of Christ. Because worship is not entertainment, there must be a restoration of the incarnational understanding of worship, that is, in worship the divine meets the human. God speaks to us in his Word. He comes to us in the sacrament. We respond in faith and go out to act on it![27]

As Webber's comment indicates, however, the renewed interest in congregational worship does not come at the expense of preaching in the church service. Rather, the new mood is an attempt to regain a more helpful balance for the sake of advancing the mandate of the church.

We embody the interaction between the individual and corporate dimensions of the life of faith in our typically evangelical emphasis on "finding a ministry in the church." We espouse the principle that each believer is to be involved in the task entrusted to the people of God, and thereby to be personally engaged in "the work of the Lord." In keeping with this concern, we encourage each church member to "find a ministry" within the context of the local fellowship. Only then can an evangelical sing with meaning, "I am happy in the service of the King."

Our interest in individual ministry within the corporate whole is likewise related to the corporate dimension of spirituality. As we engage in ministry within the company of Christ, we participate in the task of fostering spirituality in others and indirectly in ourselves. Involvement in the lives of others gives opportunity to encourage them, admonish them and meet their needs. But the goal of this is larger: that those who receive ministry may grow to spiritual maturity and in turn minister to other members of the fellowship.

This too has implications for ecclesiology. For us the church is a fellowship of believers, a fellowship of disciples, a community of persons who take seriously their own responsibility to become spiritual and at the same time conscientiously engage in the task of fostering spirituality as a corporate people. Responsible evangelicals sing together, "We will walk with each other, we will walk hand in hand." For the walk is the path of spirituality we tread individually together.

Implications for Evangelical Theology

The attempt to hold in creative tension these seemingly opposing principles points to the heart of evangelical spirituality. We understand spirituality in terms of the balanced life. The full Christian life is the product of a balance between the inward and the outward and between the individual and the corporate. Thereby we attempt to mold these dimensions into a double set of corresponding and supplementary, rather than contradictory and mutually exclusive, tendencies.

As evangelicals we understand spirituality as the inward conviction of the heart warmed by the regenerating power of the Spirit. This inward conviction, however, must be given expression by a life of discipleship in imitation of our beloved Master, the living and present Lord. Christian spirituality is an individual project, in the process of which we must dedicate all our personal resources. But it requires as well personal participation in the corporate body, the fellowship of Christ.

Our evangelical vision of spirituality is not without its flaws. Nor do we always do a good job at holding the divergent ingredients in a truly creative tension that maintains the proper balance. All too easily the balance can be lost. We can become so satisfied with testimonies of a past experience of conversion that we lose the importance of discipleship in the present; or we can quench the inner flame by mere outward adherence to dead legalisms. The evangelical emphasis on personal religion can easily lead to a schismatic individualism; or the quest for some sense of corporate unity can foster a forced uniformity.

In recent years we have begun to shift the focus of our attention away from doctrine with its focus on propositional truth in favor of a renewed interest in what constitutes the uniquely evangelical vision of spirituality.

Corresponding to this trend is a growing attempt to reformulate our evangelical self-consciousness away from the creed-based conceptions of the recent past toward an understanding based on the piety that lies deep in the broader evangelical heritage.

The implications for theology are far-reaching. This rethinking of what lies at the heart of evangelicalism demands that we evangelical theologians be careful not to focus solely on abstract doctrine. Rather, we must recapture the practical emphasis characteristic of the earlier, more pietistically inclined era in the broader history of our movement. The turn to the practical import of theology is capsuled in the old Pietist rhyme "Though Christ ten thousand times in Bethlehem were born, if he's not born in thee, thy soul's forlorn."[28] Hence to be truly evangelical, right doctrine, as important as it is, is not enough. The truth of the Christian faith must become personally experienced truth.

The renewed emphasis on the practical understanding of theology marks a shift not only to the earlier Pietism but also, in a sense, a move back from modernity to the patristic era,[29] or perhaps a move beyond modernity into the emerging postmodern era. The direct goal, if not the topic, of most patristic theological writings was the fostering of spirituality in the reader. Thus the early thinkers did not separate speculative and spiritual theology, as has been common in later eras. Only with the advent of the universities and the rise of Scholasticism did theologians begin to differentiate theology and spirituality. In the thinking of the medieval theologians, the former became a purely intellectual operation in which theological conclusions are deduced from first principles through the use of formal logic. As a consequence, the topics of the spiritual life came to be separated from theology. This trend continued until by the seventeenth century moral theology or ethics had become a separate discipline.

Of course, theology ought never to lose as its central goal the intellectual pursuit of truth viewed as the quest to understand the God who has disclosed himself in Christ. This pursuit, however, does not require the severing of intellectual from spiritual theology. On the contrary, so-called speculative theology is actually best served when theologians keep the quest for holiness in clear focus as the ultimate purpose of their task. All theological work must be directed toward the goal of fostering the spirituality of the believing community and of those engaging in the theological enterprise.

The integration of theology and spirituality, or the fostering of the practical intent of the theological enterprise, means that theology must arise out of the life of the believing community. That is, theology must flow from discipleship. Theology is not merely the intellectual findings of professional thinkers, but requisite knowledge for doers—disciples of the Lord who need to know whom they are following and why they are following him.[30] A theology that arises out of discipleship does not dismiss questions of cognition and intellectual knowing. It does not eliminate the need for a proper belief structure. But because discipleship is concerned with behavior, action and doing, the theology oriented toward discipleship constructs the Christian belief structure for the purpose of Christian living. And it claims that integral to knowing God are being and acting in conformity with God's will.

A theology rooted in spirituality, therefore, takes seriously the life of the spiritual community. As William Abraham asserts, "A true and truly Christian theology will surely be deeply rooted in revelation and tradition, in worship and prayer in the Christian community, in compassion and service in the world, in fear and trembling before the wonder of the gospel, and in humble dependence on the grace and agency of the Holy Spirit."[31]

Above all, however, a theology rooted in spirituality will be cognizant of the centrality of the doctrine of the Trinity. Ultimately, the specifically Christian spirituality finds its basis in our participation in the triune God. It is, as Houston writes, "life in the Trinity."[32] This means that believers live from the acceptance of their membership in the family of God, a status bestowed on them not by anything they have accomplished but solely by divine grace. It is theirs only by virtue of the fact that through the Holy Spirit the Son shares with them his divine relationship with the Father.

The heart of evangelicalism, therefore, lies in its vision of the Christian life. It is a religious experience couched in theological categories. The evangelical vision of Christian spirituality attempts to maintain a balance between seemingly discordant emphases. Consequently, the creative tension we attempt is no easy matter to maintain. But just this creative balance—this vision of the spiritual life and no other—is our central contribution to the people of God.

The creation of the theology that both fosters and is demanded by this vision of the faith is the task and challenge evangelicalism entrusts to those of us who are its theologians.

3
REVISIONING THE THEOLOGICAL TASK

Every Christian is a theologian. Whether consciously or unconsciously, each person of faith embraces a belief system. And each believer, whether deliberately or merely implicitly, reflects on the content of these beliefs and their significance for Christian life.

The close connection between being a Christian and theological reflection arises from the New Testament itself. The biblical documents invite the faith community to think through their beliefs in order to understand why these are a part of personal and corporate commitment (e.g., Mt 22:37; 2 Cor 10:5; 1 Pet 3:15). Theology seeks to facilitate this conscious reflection on faith. Therefore, the enterprise is to be neither feared nor despised, but rather welcomed, because of its important function within the life of discipleship.

We have asserted that the ethos of evangelicalism is a shared experience understood in terms of shared categories, a piety cradled in a theology. But what theology can assist us as evangelicals in our attempt to reflect on the faith we share?

Despite the orientation toward spirituality characteristic of the movement as a whole, contemporary evangelical thinkers generally engage in the theological task with eyes focused on epistemology or the cognitive dimension of faith, rather than toward our shared piety. Evangelical theology tends to move from the conviction that there is a deposit of cognitive revelation given once and for all in the Bible. In fact, evangelical theologians sometimes locate the genius of the movement in the combination of a material and a formal principle.[1] The material principle or content of evangelicalism encompasses the basic doctrines of the Bible, whereas the formative principle is loyalty to the Bible as the completely true and trustworthy, final and authoritative source of all doctrine. As a result, many evangelicals view the task of theology primarily as systematizing and articulating the body of doctrine they assume to preexist implicitly or explicitly in Scripture.

Klaus Bockmuehl speaks for evangelical theologians in general in declaring that the task of systematic theology "is to produce a summary of Christian doctrine, an ordered summary or synopsis of the themes of teaching in Holy Scripture. We are to collect the different, dispersed propositions on essential themes or topics of the OT and the NT and put them together in an order that fits the subject-matter in hand."[2]

Although it rightly seeks to uphold the authority of the Bible, this approach cannot serve as a catalyst for a revisioned evangelical theology. To understand this assertion, we must begin historically. We must first look at the development of theology in general and the modern evangelical propositionalism in particular. Only then can we move on to reformulate the task of an adequate evangelical theology.

The Development of Theology

The word *theology* does not appear in the biblical documents. Rather, the term originates from ancient Greece. The word is a compilation from two other Greek terms, *theos* (God) and *logos* (word, teaching, study), and therefore etymologically *theology* means "the teaching concerning, or the study of, God." The Greeks used the term to refer to the sayings of the philosophers and poets concerning divine matters, generally viewed within the framework of knowledge of humanity and nature.[3]

The Greek theological task was imported into Christian tradition early, perhaps as early as Paul's encounter with the philosophers in Athens (Acts 17:16-31), but at least by the time of the second-century Christian apologists. As late as the early Middle Ages the Greek understanding of the enterprise remained influential among Christian thinkers. They understood *theology* generally as referring to the doctrine of God, which they regarded as one topic within the broader study of dogmatics or sacred doctrine *(sacra doctrina).*[4]

During the twelfth and thirteenth centuries, however, *theology* underwent a change in meaning—from the discourse on God to the rational explication of revelation.[5] With the rise of the universities, the enterprise was destined to become an academic as well as an ecclesiastical discipline.[6] And the term came to refer to a single, unified "science" focusing on knowledge of God and having the primary character of wisdom.[7]

In eighteenth-century Germany the understanding of theology shifted again. Christian thinkers replaced the concept of a unified, practical science with the multiplicity of the theological sciences.[8] Thereby they transformed *theology* into an all-inclusive word referring to the various aspects of the study of the Bible and the church. At the same time, Christians were growing increasingly aware that the world contained a number of separate religious traditions, each with its own understanding of the divine reality. Consequently, the term came to refer to the account of God in the various religions.[9]

Today Christians generally use *theology* in a slightly narrower manner, interchangeable with what earlier thinkers termed *dogmatics*. In North America, however, this word has been replaced by "systematic theology," or more recently, "constructive" or "doctrinal theology."

Whatever the term used, the theological task encompasses the intellectual reflection on faith. Theology explores a specific religious belief system itself (doctrine). But it also focuses on the nature of believing and the integration of commitment with personal and community life. Christian theology, therefore, seeks to delineate a coherent presentation of the themes of Christian faith, which traditionally include God, human existence and the created universe, the identity of Jesus as the Christ and the salvation he brought, the Holy Spirit and the Spirit's work in the world, the church as the community expression of Christian faith, and the consummation of God's program for creation.

In the broad sense, then, we may define systematic theology as the intellectual reflection on the act, and the attempt to articulate the content, of Christian faith, including its expression in beliefs, practices and institutions.

The systematic-theological task did not arise in a vacuum. Rather, Christian theology is the product of the presence in the church of three perceived needs—polemics, catechetics and biblical summarization.[10] These factors were already visible in the early centuries of the Christian era, and in some form they continue to command attention in the church today.

The theological task grows out of the need in the church to define the Christian belief system. This intention was prominent in the early Christian centuries, when the church was faced with doctrinal controversies. Theological formulations constituted one significant aspect in the struggle to differentiate orthodoxy from heterodox views (heresy). The polemical factor was again of special importance during the Reformation era. In the face of differences over questions of faith, the various church bodies marked out their theological positions in order to define their own particular understanding of Christianity. In the modern era, the context of polemics has shifted, as Christians now sense the need to delineate the nature of their faith in the midst of many competing worldviews and religions.

The Christian theological enterprise is an outworking of the need to offer instruction to the people of God. Teaching the faith is especially important in the case of new converts, who must be instructed in the fundamentals of Christianity in order to become mature believers. To facilitate the task of teaching the many converts coming from pagan backgrounds, second-century Christian leaders developed church catechisms, which were by necessity theological in orientation. Although styles have changed, the church has continued to use theology in the fulfilling of its pedagogical mandate.

Christians have always desired to bring the basic themes and teachings of the Bible into summary form. In fact, this summarizing tendency is found already in the writings of the Bible. In the Old Testament era the Hebrew people summarized the understanding of the divine nature that arose out of their experience of God (e.g., Deut 6:4-5; 26:5-9). The New Testament likewise contains summary statements concerning topics such as the nature of salvation and the person of Christ (e.g., 1 Cor 15:3-8; Phil 2:6-11; 1 Tim 3:16). Traditionally, systematic theology has sought to bring together in systematic fashion the major biblical themes of God's gracious salvation.

Evangelical Propositionalism

As this quick survey suggests, theology as the summarization of biblical doctrine sports an impeccable pedigree within theological history. Yet the specific expression of this task among evangelicals is a relatively recent development. Many evangelical theologians elevate biblical summarization, seeing it as their central, if not sole, task, and coupling the focus on this endeavor with modern concepts of the nature of science.

Conservative theologians, whether Calvinist, dispensational, Wesleyan or Arminian, fall into step with the assumption that theology is "the science of God" based on the Bible. Just as the natural world is amenable to the scientist's probings, they argue, so also the teaching of Scripture is objectively understandable. Systematic theology organizes the "facts" of Scripture, just as the natural sciences systematize the facts of nature. Consequently, the correct theology is a crystallization of biblical truth into a set of universally true and applicable propositions.[11]

Because it champions scientific thinking, the empirical approach and common sense, George Marsden classifies evangelical theology as "early modern."[12] This characterization is surely correct. The understanding of truth and of the task of the theological discipline that characterizes much of contemporary evangelicalism predates the rise of the mid-twentieth-century coalition, having been mediated to us by the influence of the Princeton theology of the nineteenth century on the fundamentalist movement of the early twentieth. The Princeton theology had itself accepted the legacy of the older Protestant scholasticism, especially in its Reformed variety.

A theologian who is often connected with Reformed scholasticism and who through his link to the Princeton thinkers has exercised great influence on evangelicalism is Francis Turretin (1623-87). According to Turretin, the purpose of theology is to teach savingly of God.[13] To this salvific end, however, natural revelation is insufficient. Rather than being the compilation of truth disclosed in creation and discovered by reason, for Turretin theology is primarily the systematization of the teachings of Scripture,[14] and the object of theology is God as he has revealed himself in his Word.[15] Turretin's theology was likewise oriented toward propositional truth. As Richard Muller concludes, the scholasticism of the seventeenth-century Reformed thinker was an outworking of "the desire to forge a theological orthodoxy, a system of 'right-doctrine.' "[16] Turretin's legacy lies in this basic approach to theology with which his later disciples were imbued.

The approach to the task of theology set forth by Turretin was perfected by the nineteenth-century Princeton theologians. These thinkers accepted the responsibility for articulating Calvinist orthodoxy given their perception that the older theology had been rendered "so harmless that it was no longer worth believing."[17]

Although it included a pietistic strand, nineteenth-century Presbyterianism clearly emphasized biblical doctrine and the systematizing approach to the Bible influenced by the scientific paradigm of the day. Hence Charles Hodge could offer this typical comparison between science and theology:

> If natural science be concerned with the facts and laws of nature, theology is concerned with facts and principles of the Bible. If the object of the one be to arrange and systematize the facts of the external world, and to ascertain the laws by which they are determined; the object of the other is to systematize the facts of the Bible, and ascertain the prin-

ciples or general truths which those facts provide.[18]

In their doctrinal orientation the Princeton theologians were fiercely loyal to the Westminster Confession, which they believed represented the Bible's own system as closely as humanly possible.

In keeping with the emphasis on biblical doctrine, the Princeton theology elevated the propositional and unchanging nature of truth. In the characterization of Marsden, "Truth was a stable entity, not historically relative, best expressed in written language that, at least potentially, would convey one message in all times and places."[19] Hence, rather than anchoring theology in a cultural context, the Princeton thinkers sought to emancipate it from such a context, and thereby to produce a statement of truth that would be timeless and culture-free.[20] It is within this context that we are to understand Hodge's claim that during his tenure at Princeton no new idea had emerged.[21] The Princeton Presbyterians were intent on discovering and bequeathing to the church the timeless doctrinal theology found within the Bible.

The heirs of Turretin and the Princeton theologians in the evangelical tradition have generally followed the lead of their mentors in elevating biblical systematization and emphasizing the propositional nature of theological statements. Among the proponents of this biblically focused, evangelical propositionalism none has been more untiring than Carl F. H. Henry, hailed as the most prominent evangelical theologian of the second half of the twentieth century. Even without writing a systematic theology, Henry has left his mark on evangelicalism by providing the theoretical foundations for the propositionalist understanding of the theological enterprise.

One central passion of Henry's life has been the attempt to set forth the foundations for a truly valid theology. Only a return to the basic evangelical perspective can solve the current difficulty in theology, he believes. And in his understanding this basic evangelical perspective asserts that the foundation for theology can be nothing other than the revelation of God as deposited in the Scriptures.[22] Early in his tenure as founding editor of *Christianity Today,* Henry lamented "the compromise of the authority of the

Bible" noticeable in mainstream Protestantism and the "surrender of scriptural perspectives to modern critical speculations" which have led to "doubts over historical and propositional revelation, plenary inspiration, and verbal inerrancy."[23] As a result, Henry devoted himself to the defense of these dimensions of the conservative doctrine of Scripture.

The emphasis on revelation is not uniquely his, of course. But what sets Henry's brand of evangelicalism apart from other twentieth-century articulators is his understanding of the nature of revelation. According to Henry, revelation means that God has both acted in history and spoken to humankind. God's speaking is crucial to God's acting, he argues, for it provides the rationale and meaning of the divine historical acts.[24] Through God's interpretation God's activity gains meaning for us.[25] In keeping with this emphasis, Henry defines revelation as "that activity of the supernatural God whereby he communicates information essential for man's present and future destiny. In revelation God, whose thoughts are not our thoughts, shares his mind; he communicates not only the truth about himself and his intentions, but also that concerning man's present plight and future prospects."[26]

For Henry, revelation's spoken nature means that in an important way it is rational and hence propositional. In his magnum opus, the six-volume *God, Revelation and Authority,* he goes to great lengths to develop the thesis that "God's revelation is rational communication conveyed in intelligible ideas and meaningful words, that is, in conceptual-verbal form."[27] He agrees with the modern emphasis on the functional, dynamic and teleological dimensions of revelation, but argues that these cannot be separated from the propositional. For him, the reality that God has spoken means that the intellect plays an integral role in the revelatory process.[28] Revelation, in other words, is objective,[29] conceptual,[30] intelligible and coherent.[31] Therefore Christianity, rather than being an escape from rationality, is oriented toward the intellect.[32]

Lying behind the rational character of the Christian faith Henry finds "the rational living God"[33] who "addresses man in his Word."[34] The Christian revelation, therefore, is "rationally consistent and compelling," for "rationality has its very basis in the nature of the Living God."[35] The concepts of revelation, reason and Scripture coalesce in Henry's basic epistemological axiom:

> Divine revelation is the source of all truth, the truth of Christianity included; reason is the instrument for recognizing it; Scripture is its verifying principle; logical consistency is a negative test for truth and coherence a subordinate test. The task of Christian theology is to exhibit the content of biblical revelation as an orderly whole.[36]

The emphasis on the propositional dimension of revelation so prominent in Henry's thought finds its supplement in his anthropology. In keeping with the rationalist tradition in theology, Henry elevates reason to the status of being the foundational dimension of the human person—a view, he argues, that was universally held prior to the modern era.[37] In fact, he finds in the biblical concept of the image of God the explanation for the phenomenon of divine revelation.[38] Despite the Fall, this divine image (which Henry views as including a certain knowledge of God, rational competence and ethical accountability) was present in some measure in every human being.[39]

Although acknowledging the presence of the divine image in everyone and the doctrinal importance of general revelation,[40] Henry argues that theology can be based only on the self-disclosure of God found in the Bible. In this way, he sets himself apart from evangelical "evidentialists," those apologists who seek to ground Christian faith on arguments from reason and empirical evidence. Henry follows the "presuppositionalist" approach,[41] basing all theology solely on the presupposition of the truthfulness of the Bible,[42] which he understands as presenting the truth of God in propositional form.

All evangelicals owe a debt of gratitude to Carl Henry. His erudition as a defender of biblical authority in the modern world is unquestioned. His mammoth *God, Revelation and Authority* has set both a standard and an agenda for younger evangelical theologians. Above all, his restatement of the classical concordance model of theology may be lauded and debated long after his departure from the theological scene.

Despite its uncontestable importance to evangelicalism, the "concordance" model of systematic theology implicit in Turretin, propounded by Hodge and developed into evangelical propositionalism by thinkers such as Henry has not been without its detractors. In one sense, the entire thrust of modern theology since Schleiermacher has sought to provide a viable alternative to the tradition out of which propositionalism developed—the focus on authoritatively communicated truths—without opting for its Enlightenment alternative, which elevated the quest for truths gained through the speculative reason.[43]

More devastating than the implicit critique leveled by the developing liberal tradition, however, was that of twentieth-century neo-orthodoxy. The repeated outcry of neo-orthodox thinkers has been that revelation does not disclose supernatural knowledge—a body of propositions about God. Rather, in revelation, God himself encounters the human person.[44]

Evangelical theologians have rightly responded to the critique of neo-orthodoxy by refusing to acknowledge the disjunction between propositional and personal revelation.[45] Revelation, they argue, is both. While acknowledging that neo-orthodoxy is correct in asserting that what God primarily does is reveal himself, evangelicals add that God does so at least in part by telling us something about himself. And this *something* takes the form of propositions.

In spite of helpful responses such as these, the challenges posed by nonevangelical critics have led certain evangelical thinkers in recent years to grow uneasy with the older view.

Some voices within the movement have called for only minor refinements. Ronald Nash, for example, advocates a mere cosmetic, terminological change. Noting that the label "propositional revelation" was probably not coined by evangelicals, he finds no "sentimental reason" for continuing to use it. "Instead of an alliterative formula," he writes, "evangelicals should simply insist that some revelatory acts have a cognitive or informational character, and that this revealed truth is inscripturated in the several different literary forms found in the Bible."[46]

More germane is the critique articulated by John Jefferson Davis. He reflects the opinion of many when he faults the older evangelical approach for not taking "adequate account of the social context of the theological task and the historicity of all theological reflection." Davis claims that this approach "tends to promote a repetition of traditional formulations of biblical doctrine, rather than appropriate recontextualizations of the doctrines in response to changing cultural and historical conditions."[47]

In keeping with this concern, an entire cadre of evangelical theologians are now urging each other to contextualize their theology.[48] This is evident, for example, in Millard Erickson's definition of theology as "that discipline which strives to give a coherent statement of the doctrines of the Christian faith, based primarily upon the Scriptures, placed in the context of culture in general, worded in a contemporary idiom, and related to issues of life."[49] Similarly, Richard J. Gehman advocates a contextualizing theology, which he defines as that dynamic process whereby the people of God living in community and interacting with believers throughout time and space, under the illuminating guidance of the Holy Spirit, proclaim in their own language and thought-forms the Word that God has spoken to them in their context through the study of Scripture.[50]

Other evangelicals, however, have not been satisfied that either contextualization or a mere adjustment in terminology is sufficient. They are convinced that more radical measures are needed if the evangelical theological experiment is to be salvaged. Clark Pinnock, for example, rejects as inflexible and undynamic the "propositional theology that sees its function as imposing systematic rationality on everything it encounters."[51] Taking his cue from the contemporary narrative outlook, he chides academic theology for looking for truth in doctrine rather than in the biblical story. Viewing revelation as primarily narrative, Pinnock sees the task of theology as expounding the story and explicating its meanings. Theology, then, is a secondary language whose propositions "live off the power of the primary story."[52]

The call to move beyond mere contextualization, as helpful and necessary as this endeavor may be, is surely correct. Despite good intentions, evangelical contextualizers all too easily can remain trapped in a view of propositional revelation that simply equates the divine self-disclosure with the Bible and that propounds an understanding of how the Bible in its canonical form came into existence that, as we will see in chapter five, is no longer viable. These theologians are likewise at risk of merely continuing the older enterprise of biblical summarization, with only a slight nod to the necessity of rephrasing theological propositions in contemporary language.

Despite his progressive call for contextualization, Erickson occasionally displays this conservative tendency. For example, after bemoaning the neo-orthodox fixation on personal revelation, he gives indication that he himself has not broken out of the fixation on timeless, universal propositions so characteristic of the older propositionalism. He writes, "If revelation includes propositional truths, then it is of such a nature that it can be preserved. It can be written down or *inscripturated.*"[53] From this declaration he then moves to delineate the traditional doctrine of inspiration.

The shift to narrative, while not providing the entire answer, does mark a helpful beginning point. We must view theology in terms of its proper context within the narrative of God's action in history. This means that the theological task can be properly pursued only "from within"—that is, only from the vantage point of the faith community in which the theologian stands.

Theology, Faith and the Faith Community

Despite its shortcomings, evangelical propositionalism capsules a fundamental insight. Our faith is tied to the truth content of a divine revelation that has been objectively disclosed. God has communicated truth—himself—to us.

The difficulty with evangelical propositionalism, therefore, is not its acknowledgment of a cognitive dimension of revelation and consequently of the statements of theology. Indeed, the doctrines explored by the theologian are surely more than "noninformative and nondiscursive symbols of inner feelings, attitudes, or existential orientation," to employ George Lindbeck's description of the "experiential-expressive" dimension of religion.[54]

Instead, the problem with evangelical propositionalism is its often under-developed understanding of how the cognitive dimension functions within the larger whole of revelation. Therefore evangelical theologians tend to misunderstand the social nature of theological discourse. More than its advocates have cared to admit, evangelical theology has been the captive of the orientation to the individual knower that has reigned over the Western mindset throughout the modern era. But this orientation is now beginning to lose its grip. Therefore, if our theology is to speak the biblical message in our contemporary situation, we must shed the cloak of modernity and reclaim the more profound community outlook in which the biblical people of God were rooted.

The revisioning of the theological task is dependent on a renewed understanding of the role of the community in the life of faith. Evangelicals are correct in asserting that the revealed truth of God forms the "basic grammar" that creates Christian identity. Rather than merely being a product of our experience, as certain strands of liberalism have tended to argue, in an important sense the truth of God *creates* our experience.[55] But this identity-creative process is not an individualistic matter occurring in isolation. Instead, it is a development that happens within a community.

Voices within the human sciences, not evangelical theologians, have served as the pioneers in the contemporary attempt to move beyond a focus on the autonomous individual. Thinkers in a wide variety of disciplines have been exploring the thesis that personal identity is formed within social structures. There is an intricate web of traditions and beliefs by which we understand ourselves and shape our lives, they theorize. To the degree that it provides the categories or language in which we frame our questions and answers, we are shaped by this inherited web. The transmitting agency that mediates the web of belief to us is the social group or community within which the ongoing process of identity formation occurs.[56]

At stake in the new outlook, therefore, is a more profound understanding of epistemology. Recent thinking has helped us see that the process of knowing, and to some extent even the process of experiencing the world, can occur only within a conceptual framework, a framework mediated by the social community in which we participate.

The application of this understanding to the religious dimension of life follows. Foundational to our self-identity, religion claims, is religious experience—an experience of or encounter with the divine. This experience, as well as the conceptual framework that facilitates it, is mediated by the religious community—through its symbols, narratives and sacred documents—in which we participate.

We must be careful, therefore, not to focus our understanding of religious experience only on an individual-centered paradigm of the divine-human encounter. Although coming in the purview of the individual believer, religious experience is also corporate in nature. In fact, there is a sense of primacy in this corporate experience of encounter with the divine reality. In the biblical tradition, the goal of the human-divine encounter is to constitute a community of people in covenant with God. The Christian church declares that we enter that community through a faith response to the proclamation of the salvific action of God in Christ, symbolized by baptism.

The implications for theology of this understanding of the relationship of the community to individual faith formation are immense. In fact, it has launched a revolution in thinking concerning the task of theology. The ideal that predominated during both the medieval and modern eras viewed theology as a systematic investigation of the range of Christian doctrine, coupled with the attempt to demonstrate the truth of the Christian faith for the entire panorama of human knowledge. In the evangelical movement, this ideal took the form of the isolated scholar seeking to systematize the deposit of truth found in the Bible.

Today the older ideal is losing ground to an emphasis on theology as directed toward a "practical" purpose—that is, as related to the life and practice of the Christian community. Through the recounting of the biblical narrative of God's salvific action in Israel and preeminently in Christ, the Christian community fulfills a mediating function in the lives of its members. The biblical narrative builds the conceptual framework by which the community views itself and its experience of the world. Theology, in turn, functions within the context of the Christian community by reflecting on its conceptual framework and belief structure.

The newer understanding of theology as "practical" parallels developments in several of the human sciences. For example, it reflects points of contact with Niklas Luhmann's sociology of theology. According to Luhmann, theology is the self-reflection of religion, and as such it is instrumental to the maintenance of the identity of that religion.[57]

Similar to Luhmann, the German theologian Gerhard Sauter, among others, views the primary task of theology as critical reflection on the life and practice of the church, in order to exercise a critiquing and norming function in contemporary church discourse and life.[58] The same point is made by Ronald Thiemann, who declares that the goal of theology is "to understand more fully and more critically the Christian faith in order that the community might better exemplify the Christian identity to which it has been called."[59] So forceful have been recent voices setting forth the fundamentally practical nature of theology that Peter Slater finds a consensus among theologians that their discipline "serves the faithful, whether as individuals or collectives, and it does so properly when it enables them *to live* more faithfully."[60]

One implication of the focus on the practical task of theology is the realization that theological discourse is a second-order discipline pursued "from within." The enterprise is a critical, reflective activity that presupposes the beliefs and practices of the Christian community. The theologian, consequently, speaks from the perspective of a personal faith commitment and participation in the life of the community.

The newer thinking suggests that our search for a new evangelical paradigm must begin with the community of faith. To understand theology properly, we must view it within the context of the life of the people of God. Theology is indeed the task of the faith community. We need no other rationale to engage in the discipline than our presence and participation in the Christian community. And our endeavors are fundamentally, even if not totally, directed back toward that community.

These considerations suggest that we may view theology as the faith community's reflecting on the faith experience of those who have encountered God through the divine activity in history and therefore now seek to live as the people of God in the contemporary world. Ultimately, then, the propositions of systematic theology find their source and aim in the identity and life of the community it serves. As Theodore Jennings notes, "Theological reflection is always reflection on behalf of . . . on behalf of a community, on behalf of a tradition, on behalf of a world."[61]

How does the Bible fit into this schema? It goes without saying that the Christian community finds the Bible crucial to its task of being the covenant people and living out its calling. But how are we to understand the relationship between Scripture and theology understood as a practical discipline? Although the fuller exposition of a "revisioned" position must await chapter five, a few summary points are in order here.

The answer to this query lies in the conjunction between theology and revelation. Theology has always been viewed as in some way closely connected to and dependent on revelation. Evangelical thinkers, following the tradition of Protestant scholasticism from Turretin to Hodge, link revelation with Scripture, and consequently they view theology as the systemization of the propositional truth disclosed in the Bible. Neo-orthodoxy agrees that theology is the reflection on revelation, but differs from evangelicalism in its understanding of where such revelation can be found. Neo-orthodox theologians argue that this revelation lies in God's personal self-disclosure, rather than in the propositional truth gleaned from the Scriptures.

As we will argue in chapter five, neither the classic evangelical nor the neo-orthodox position has proved ultimately satisfying. Both are hampered by their emphasis on the individual knower. Revelation, in contrast, is an event that has occurred in the community within which the believing individual stands. "The revelation of God" is the divine act of self-disclosure, which reveals nothing less than the essence of God. This divine self-disclosure, while standing ultimately at the eschaton—at the end of history—is nevertheless a present reality, for it has appeared proleptically in history. On the basis of Karl Barth's identification of the dependent relationship between the inscripturated word and the Word incarnate, we must view the revelation in history in terms of the process of community formation arising out of the paradigmatic events that stand at its genesis.

The Christian community, emerging as it did out of the older Hebrew trajectory of community formation, was and continues to be constituted by the central events of the biblical narrative. In the New Testament, the church preserved the memory of those grand foundational events together with the earliest responses to the revelation of God in Christ, which it understood in the light and context of the Old Testament. Through the interaction of each succeeding generation with the biblical documents, the paradigmatic events and the early confrontation with these events become a continual source of revelation for the ongoing life of the community. Scripture is the foundational record of how the ancient faith community responded in the context of a trajectory of historical situations to the awareness that God has acted to constitute this people as a covenant community. In this way the Bible stands as the informing and forming canon for the community throughout its history.

Theology is related to these paradigmatic events, as well as to their historical and ongoing use in the community of faith. The task of theology is to assist the contemporary believing community to fulfill its responsibility of proclaiming and living out the message that God has appeared in Christ for the sake of the salvation of humankind. Theology assists in this enterprise as it focuses its attention on the community's confession of faith. To this end it raises the central questions concerning faith: What does it mean to be the community of those who confess faith in the God revealed in Jesus of Nazareth? And how are we to verbalize and embody that confession in the contemporary context? The clarification of these queries on behalf of the church is the role of theology.

To this end, theology functions in a manner similar to Lindbeck's characterization of church doctrine. Taking what he terms a "cultural-linguistic" approach to conceptualizing religion, Lindbeck sees doctrine as providing a "regulative" function.[62] For the individual believer, the believing community provides a cultural and linguistic framework that shapes life and thought. More than being molded by the experiences of individuals within it, the communal reality constitutes a central factor in the shaping of the subjectivities and experiences of its members. It provides a constellation of symbols and concepts which its members employ in order to understand their lives and experiences of the world and within which they experience their world.[63] Taking Lindbeck's idea a step further, we conclude that theology systematizes, explores and orders the community symbols and concepts into a unified whole—that is, into a systematic conceptual framework.

Hence, theology is a second-order enterprise, and its propositions are second-order propositions.[64] Theology formulates in culturally conditioned language the confession and worldview of the community of faith—of that people who have been constituted by the human response to the story of the salvific act of God in the history of Jesus the Christ.

The assertion that theology speaks a second-order language is not intended to deny the ontological nature of theological declarations. Nevertheless, the ontological claims implicit in theological assertions arise as an outworking of the intent of the theologian to provide a model of reality, rather than to describe reality directly.

The abiding ontological dimension of theological assertions raises an important caution. We dare not conclude from the emphasis on the practical nature of theology that the theologian can now retreat from the public discussion of ultimate truth. The focus on the practical nature of theology does not automatically lead to a new subjectivity; it does not aim to replace the subjectivity of the knowing subject with a subjectivity of the isolated believing community. In this context, the philosophical work of Michael Polanyi is illuminating.[65]

Polanyi claims that our location within the social milieu of a particular place and time is not a liability. Rather, it forms the opportunity for pursuing truth, for although our thought emerges from particular circumstances, it is not limited to them. Further, he argues that all thought strives for truth. But because truth cannot be subjective in either an individual or a social sense, this striving for truth carries a "universal intent." However, he cautions against confusing this *concern for* universality with any *claim about* universality. For Polanyi truth always transcends our apprehension of it, and this drives us ever onward in the search for truth. For belief involves compelling orientations to which our formulations and propositions give only approximate expression. On this basis, Polanyi argues that all forms of positivism (which focuses on the propositions themselves as expressing final truth) represent a truncated view of belief.

The contemporary situation demands that we as evangelicals not view theology merely as the restatement of a body of propositional truths, as important as doctrine is. Rather, theology is a practical discipline oriented primarily toward the believing community. Polanyi's theses suggest that this situation does not necessarily prevent theologians from raising the truth question. On the contrary, our participation in a faith community involves a basic commitment to a specific conceptual framework. Because faith is linked to a conceptual framework, our participation in a community of faith carries a claim to truth, even if that claim be merely implicit. By its very nature, the conceptual framework of a faith community claims to represent in some form the truth about the world and the divine reality its members have come to know and experience.

To the extent that it embodies the conceptual framework of a faith community, therefore, theology necessarily engages in the quest for truth. It enters into conversation with other disciplines of human knowledge with the goal of setting forth a Christian worldview that coheres with what we know about human experience in the world. To this end, theology seeks to understand the human person and the world as existing in relationship to the reality of God, and in so doing to fashion a fuller vision of God and God's purposes in the world.[66]

The practical and veracious dimensions of the theological enterprise, therefore, are not two disjointed, competing tasks. Rather, they form one interconnected whole. Consequently, we need not agree with his emphasis on "feeling" to applaud Delwin Brown's conclusion concerning the task of theology:

> Religious peoples, Christians and others, inhabit what we might call worlds of felt meaning. That is, our traditions create, sustain, and transform us primarily in the felt dimensions of our personal and corporate

lives together—in our worship, in our relationship to our canons, in shared patterns of action, and in our common sensibilities. Theological systems attempt to portray the meaning of these felt worlds in reflective, coherent conceptualities. And in part because each religious world does cohere at a felt level our theological portrayals of them also hang together internally (just as they in turn . . . must connect up consistently with what we say about the world scientifically, historically, aesthetically, etc.).[67]

Likewise, although James McClendon may be somewhat obscure, he is nevertheless on the right track in defining theology as the "discovery, understanding, and transformation of the convictions of a convictional community, including the discovery and critical revision of their relation to one another *and to whatever else there is.*"[68]

The Nature of Theology

With this description of theology's connection to the believing community in view, we are in a position to delineate more clearly and systematically the nature of theology itself. The goal of our discussion demands that we introduce several of the traditional questions concerning how we are to understand theology and that we view theology in terms of certain related concepts.

Central to such an exploration is the question of how we are to understand theology in comparison to faith. Although intimately related, theology and personal faith differ in certain ways. Faith is by nature immediate. Christian faith arises out of the human encounter with the person of God in Christ, mediated by the faith community's testimony to the divine revelation in Jesus. Faith, therefore, is the personal response to the call of God—and this response involves our presence in a believing community.

The response of faith is all-encompassing, extending to all aspects of a person's being. It includes an intellectual aspect, for in faith we accept as true certain assertions concerning reality, and as a result we view the world in a specific way. Faith includes a volitional aspect, for it entails the commitment of ourselves to Another, the God revealed in Jesus Christ, and consequently in a certain sense to the community of the disciples of Jesus.

Theology, in contrast, is the believing community's intellectual reflection on faith. It is the attempt to approach faith as a subject for discussion and reflection in order to illumine and understand it. The focus of the theologians' questions, then, is faith: To what statements do we give assent—that is, what propositions do we accept as reflecting the nature of reality? What is the nature of personal commitment, or what does it mean to commit oneself? To whom are we committing ourselves, or what is the object of our faith? In other words, insofar as theology is reflection on faith, it seeks to isolate the specifically intellectual aspect of faith and then to articulate, clarify and develop this aspect.

The distinction between faith and theology confirms that theology is a second-order endeavor. It is called forth by faith, as Christians seek to reflect on the reality of faith.

The relation between theology and faith also indicates that theology must not be confused with the intellectual discipline known as religious studies, which entails the study of systems of religious belief. In approaching their subject matter, students of religious studies emphasize, as far as possible, objective observation and detached work. Scholars in religious studies seek to work "from the outside," apart from personal adherence to the belief system under study. Theology, however, while not totally devoid of detached work and objective observation, consists of reflection on faith within the context of the believing community. Its observations are conducted from within the faith stance and the faith community. Theology expresses the nature and content of faith from a sympathetic, committed viewpoint. Thus, in contrast to students of religious studies, theologians do not seek to free themselves from their own faith commitments and their faith community. Rather, they begin with a sympathetic attitude toward the religious tradition in which they stand.

Faith, then, is the key to the difference between theology and religious studies. Theoretically, anyone could engage in the latter, whereas the theological task is limited to persons of faith. Anyone can study Buddhism or Christianity. But no one can be a Buddhist theologian without being a

Buddhist, or claim to be a Christian theologian without participating in the Christian tradition. Christian theology seeks to articulate the specifically Christian understanding of reality, one that views the world through the eyes of faith in the God revealed through Jesus.

While theology pulls into its purview reality as a whole and seeks to describe reality from the viewpoint of faith, no theological system ought to be seen as encompassing reality in its fullness. The reality it studies—God, the human person and the world as a whole—can never be fully grasped by the human intellect. Therefore every theological construct will have limitations. At the same time, the human mind can grasp *something* concerning reality. Theology seeks to facilitate this task by the use of models.

Important to our understanding of the role of models in the theological enterprise is the differentiation between replica and analogue models found in contemporary philosophy of science. Whereas replica models strive to replicate the modeled reality on a smaller, more easily visualized scale, analogue models attempt to simulate the structural relationships of the reality modeled. The model constructed by theology is of the latter type rather than the former.[69] A theological system does not provide a "scale model" of reality. Its statements are not univocal. Rather, it seeks to invoke an understanding of reality by speaking in an analogous fashion about matters that may be mysterious, even ineffable.

No theological system can claim to be a scale model, an exact verbal reproduction of the nature of God, the human person or the world. Nevertheless, a systematic theology can be helpful, insofar as it is an analogue model designed to assist the human spirit in grasping truth concerning reality. Christian theology is an attempt to speak about the world by focusing on the significance of Jesus of Nazareth for creation and history. It seeks to assist the Christian community in articulating the importance for all human life of Jesus Christ, and the importance of a faith commitment to Jesus as the Christ. To this end it constructs an analogue model of reality viewed from the vantage point of commitment to the God revealed in Jesus.

Our theology, of course, is specifically and unabashedly "Christian." Hence our theological model must always remain "orthodox." It will seek to capsule the vision of a world under God which has always stood at the center of the faith of the people of God. In this sense, theology may be seen as "retroduction," the delineation of a conceptual model of reality that is informed by the Scriptures and by the theological heritage of the church.

At the same time, as many evangelical theologians have pointed out in recent years, theology must always be a contextual discipline. Rather than merely amplifying, refining, defending and handing on a timeless, fixed orthodoxy, theologians, speaking from within the community of faith, seek to describe the act of faith, the One toward whom faith is directed and the implications of our faith commitment in, for and to a specific historical and cultural context. For this reason, the categories we employ in our theology are by necessity culturally and historically conditioned, and as theologians each of us is both a "child of the times" and a communicator to the times.

Because the community of faith is to be a faithful people in history, the people of God experience a creative tension between loyalty to their affirmation of faith and the culture in which they dwell. But because this cultural context changes in differing times and places, the theologian's task of seeking to assist the church in relating the Word of God to the varied, changing flow of human thought and life never comes to an end. Theology is always *in transitu,* and the theologian is a pilgrim thinker working on behalf of a pilgrim people.[70]

As a contextual discipline theology performs the function of an "intermediator." From their vantage point within the Christian tradition, theologians seek to assist the church in bringing the affirmation of faith, "Jesus is Lord," into the contemporary context. Theology articulates this affirmation in the thought-forms of the culture of the community it serves and shows its implications, relevance and application to life in that society and that place in history. Although the fundamental Christian faith-commitment to God through Christ is unchanging, the world into which this commitment is to be brought is in flux. The theologian serves the church in each generation and each cultural setting by helping the people of God to articulate their faith and apply it to the world in which they live.

This understanding suggests several dangers that confront us as Christian theologians. The first potential pitfall arises from the temptation to substitute personal theologizing for a genuine faith commitment. We can easily replace commitment to the living Christ, for example, with our doctrines concerning Christ. Likewise, we run the risk of placing our confidence in our abilities to develop a theological system, rather than in the God in whose service we stand. A related temptation is to move away from theology into religious studies. As theologians we can become so objective in the discipline that we lose from view our personal faith commitment to the Christ on whom our vocation centers. In this way we fall prey to eventually reducing Christianity to the status of one religion among others.

Second, as Christian theologians we run the risk of confusing one specific model of reality with reality itself, or one theological system with truth itself. Although present among persons of all persuasions, this "canonization" of a particular theological construct is especially problematic among conservative thinkers, for we have a tendency to elevate a specific theologian of the past or the present to the status of "doctor of the church." Because all systems are only models of reality—albeit informed by Scripture and by the mileposts of theological history—we must maintain a stance of openness to other models, being aware of the tentativeness and incompleteness of all such systems. In the final analysis, theology is a human enterprise—helpful for the task of the church, to be sure, but a human construct nevertheless.

Finally, as Christian theologians we are tempted to see our task as ending with the construction of a theological system. In actuality, devising a "system," however important this may be, is not our ultimate goal. Rather, as theologians we engage in articulating faith, in order that the life of each believer and of the faith community in the world might be served. Our theological reflection ought to make a difference in Christian living. Doctrinal expression is designed to help clarify the ways in which Christian commitment is to be lived. It likewise ought to help motivate all Christians to live in accordance with their commitment.

In short, our theology must overflow into ethics. Whenever theology stops short of this, it has failed to be obedient to its calling.

Michael Goldberg is on the right track when he concludes from his recounting of the story of Augustine, "Though a propositional theology may have its place, that place is limited by life itself, for as its propositions are abstracted and drawn from life, so too, in the end, they must return to life and have meaning for life in order to be theologically significant."[71]

In the same way, we need not go all the way with Lindbeck in discounting the ontological intent of theological descriptions to agree with his main point: "The primary focus is not on God's being in itself, for that is not what the text is about, but on how life is to be lived and reality construed in the light of God's character as an agent as this is depicted in the stories of Israel and of Jesus."[72]

A revisioned evangelical theology seeks to reflect on the faith commitment of the believing community in order to construct a model of reality. This model in turn aims to foster a truly evangelical spirituality that translates into ethical living in the social-historical context in which we are called to be the people of God.

But what principles form the sources for such a revisioned evangelical theology? It is to this question that we now turn our attention.

4
REVISIONING THE SOURCES FOR THEOLOGY

Twentieth-century postfundamentalist evangelical theology has tended to take a propositionalist approach to the theological enterprise. The task of theology so conceived is the discovery of the one doctrinal system that inheres in the Bible. This approach entails one great contribution: an unbending affirmation that God has disclosed truth to humankind.

The revisioned evangelical theology advocated in these chapters views the theological task in a slightly different fashion. It conceives theology as reflection on the faith commitment of the believing community. This theology aims to construct a model of reality that is in keeping with the biblical message and the historic position of the faith community, and that can foster a truly evangelical spirituality that translates into ethical living in the social-historical context in which we are called to be the people of God.

Consequently, one crucial goal of a revisioned evangelical theology is to move beyond the solely propositionalist paradigm, while maintaining its central affirmation. Evangelical theologians ought to move away from conceiving their task as merely to discover divinely disclosed truth understood as the single, unified doctrinal system purportedly lodged within the pages of the Bible and waiting to be categorized and systematized. Although to some degree systematization does belong to our overarching program, our task is not simply the explication of this one, true scriptural system of doctrine. Rather, it has a distinctively practical intent.

Let us not conclude, however, that the proposed shift in understanding of the nature and task of theology discounts the role of the Bible for the church or for the theologian. On the contrary, our revisioned theology must take into full consideration the historic evangelical assertion that the Bible is the authoritative book of the faith community. What the new theological paradigm requires is a revisioned understanding of the *nature* of the Bible's authority. To anticipate the conclusions of chapter five, Scripture functions authoritatively as the source for the symbols, stories, teachings and doctrines that form the cognitive framework for the worldview of the believing community. And theology, in turn, is the systematic, intellectual articulation of that worldview, its underlying symbols and its import for the church in a given historical-cultural context.

Given this task of theology, three further questions arise. The first query focuses on the resources the theologian employs. The second asks concerning the actual role of the Bible as our authority in theology. And the third searches for an integrating motif for an evangelical theology that can serve contemporary needs. The present chapter takes up the first of these two questions, that of the sources for theology. The authority of Scripture is the topic of chapter five. And the quest for a theological motif is elaborated in chapter six.

Traditional Sources for Evangelical Theology
The theological enterprise, focusing as it does on the intellectual reflection

on faith, does not arise *sui generis* (out of itself). Nor does the theologian engage in this task without the aid of resources. Rather, the theologian acknowledges certain norms, which function as the specific sources he or she utilizes in carrying out the theological mandate.

Traditionally, evangelicals have self-consciously endeavored to construct systematic theologies largely or exclusively on only one foundation—the Bible. This approach corresponds naturally to the evangelical understanding of the essential discovery made in the Reformation, which we look to as constituting the initial formative stage of the movement. As evangelicals we view *sola scriptura* as one of the central advancements of the sixteenth-century Reformation, and consequently we see this principle as foundational to our own theological method.

The emphasis on *sola scriptura* was the outworking of the Reformers' attempt to correct what they saw as the methodological errors of medieval theology. The theologians of the Roman Catholic church looked to two major sources for correct doctrine or dogma. Together these constituted a twofold source of truth. The first, of course, was the Bible—more specifically, the Bible as canonized by the church and as interpreted by the magisterium, the church's teaching office. The second fount of truth according to the medieval theorists was apostolic tradition as handed down through, and even augmented by, the church.

The Reformers resolutely rejected the twofold source for theological truth. Martin Luther set forth a simpler approach focusing on *sola scriptura* (Scripture alone). Through this slogan he meant to assert that Scripture—not the Bible plus tradition—is the primary source for theology. Later the Calvinists, especially the English Puritans, refined Luther's position. The Westminster Confession of Faith, for example, which forms the apex of Puritan efforts to delineate a proper recounting of biblical doctrine, declares that the authority in the church is the working together of two principles—Scripture and the Holy Spirit.[1] Hence, the Puritans understood Luther's axiom of *sola scriptura* as meaning that the source of doctrine is the Spirit speaking through the Scriptures.

In recent years, some evangelical thinkers have sought to augment the theological heritage of the Reformation. Their goal is the incorporation into the traditional commitment to *sola scriptura* an explicit concern for the contextualizing of theology. The commitment to contextualization, however, entails an implicit rejection of the older evangelical conception of theology as the construction of truth on the basis of the Bible alone. No longer can the theologian focus merely on Scripture as the one complete theological norm. Instead, the process of contextualization requires a movement between two poles—the Bible as the source of truth and the culture as the source of the categories through which the theologian expresses biblical truth. Of course, Scripture remains the primary source and norm for theological statements. Nevertheless, contextualization demands that the theologian take seriously the thought-forms and mindset of the culture in which theologizing transpires, in order to explicate the eternal truths of the Scriptures in language that is understandable to contemporary people.

The appeal to Bible and culture in the completion of the theological task is, of course, not unique to evangelical methodology. In fact, perhaps the most erudite twentieth-century articulation of this approach is the well-known method of correlation proposed by Paul Tillich. Tillich's approach focuses on the existential questions posed by philosophy and the revelatory answers set forth by theology. Through careful examination of human existence, the theologian employs philosophy in order to raise the grave questions encountered by humans today. Then he or she draws on the symbols of divine revelation to formulate answers to the questions implied in human existence, which philosophy can discover but not answer. According to Tillich, therefore, the overall task of the theologian is to bring the questions and answers together in critical correlation.[2] The answers theology presents must be derived from revelation, but they must be expressed in a form that will speak to the existential concerns of human beings. Consequently, the theologian's goal is to articulate the answers of revelation in a manner that remains faithful to the original Christian message while being relevant to the questions asked by the modern, secular mindset.

In recent years, yet another methodology has gained increasing support, even among evangelicals.[3] This approach is often termed "the Wesleyan quadrilateral," because it purports to find its genesis in John Wesley.[4] Theology, proponents declare, appeals to four sources: Scripture (the Bible as properly exegeted), reason (the findings of science and human reasoning), experience (individual and corporate encounters with life) and tradition (the teachings of the church throughout its history).[5]

One recent evangelical convert to the Wesleyan view, Clark Pinnock, orders and characterizes the four sources as "a written form [of revelation] (Scripture), a remembering community (tradition), a process of subjective appropriation (experience), and testing for internal consistency (reason)."[6] Pinnock cautions that these sources must be held in "creative tension as responding in their different ways to the revelation of God." Each of the four is vital; therefore, no one source is to be overemphasized to the exclusion of the others.[7]

Although affirming all four as valid, Wesleyan theologians tend to elevate one or another of the points of the quadrilateral above the others. In the attempt to maintain the Reformation tradition, for example, conservative or evangelical Wesleyans appeal to the Bible as the "norming norm," the source which stands above the others.[8] Liberal Wesleyans, on the other hand, may elevate either experience or reason.

The Wesleyan quadrilateral is not without problems. Perhaps its gravest difficulty lies in its appeal to experience as constituting a theological norm separate from the others. A criticism of any methodology that elevates experience as a theological norm was voiced already by Paul Tillich. In a well-known dictum, he rightly declared that experience is not the source of theology but rather the medium through which theology's sources are received.[9]

Connected with Tillich's observation are several additional considerations, which likewise weigh against the assertion that experience is a separate source for theology. For example, rather than being its source, experience is better seen as in some sense the focus of the theological task. Theology is the reflection on faith, which as an act and as carrying implications for living is by its own nature experiential. Theologians utilize the proper theological sources in order to construct an interpretive framework or grid to assist in organizing and understanding our experience. Theology, then, is in some sense the critical reflection on Christian experience, for it seeks to describe and account for the experience of faith in accordance with specifically Christian categories.[10]

Carrying this consideration a step further, experience cannot form a separate source simply because we never receive experience uninterpreted. It is always filtered by an interpretive framework or worldview grid. In fact, the framework facilitates the reception of experience, for there is no "pure experience." This being the case, experience cannot serve as a source for theology separate from the worldview that makes its reception possible.

Contemporary thinkers are moving in the direction of a consensus concerning this critical appraisal of experience.[11] According to Francis Fiorenza, for example, experience is primarily an act of interpretation that occurs within the context of cultural history and therefore is embedded in a cultural tradition.[12] Similarly, George Lindbeck argues that language and symbol are necessary preconditions for experience, and hence religions produce experience rather than merely being the expressions of it. This means that a valid theological proposal may contradict previous experience, transform present experience and facilitate future experience.

Finally, experience cannot be a proper source for theology because any appeal to an unreflective individual experience is by nature wholly subjective. It lacks any canon by means of which it can be judged, both as to whether it is real or imagined and as to whether it is positive or negative, good or evil. Experience also leaves open the question of universalizability: is such an experience normative for all, or is it merely a private, individual phenomenon?

One caution is important here, however. The rejection of experience as a separate norm for theology does not mean that it is irrelevant to the theological enterprise.[13] Because we dare not confuse our experience of God with our relationship to God, the human experience of God is not the only object of the theologian's inquiry. Nevertheless, our experience is informative; it does help us clarify the human relation to God. For this reason, experience stands as an important dimension in the theological task.

The Wesleyan quadrilateral, like the viewpoints it is designed to supersede, does not provide the final answer to the question concerning the sources for theology. Rather than looking to one, two or four sources, the evangelical theological structure must be supported by three pillars. We must, therefore, employ three norms as we do theology.

The Three Pillars of Theology

As the attempt to articulate the unchanging faith commitment of the church—the Christian confession "Jesus is Lord"—in a specific historical-cultural context, the theological task must be carried out with a view in three directions. The three "pillars" or norms of theology form an ordered sequence of (1) the biblical message, (2) the theological heritage of the church and (3) the thought-forms of the historical-cultural context in which the contemporary people of God seek to speak, live and act.[14]

Of first importance to the theological task is the Bible as canonized by the church. More specifically, the primary norm for theology is the biblical message. The theologian must look first and above all to the kerygma as inscripturated in the Bible. Theology must always take seriously the good news as proclaimed within the context of the ancient cultures—that is, the trajectory of the proclamation of the story of God's salvific activity within the history of Israel, Jesus and the infant church.

The primacy of the biblical kerygma in the theological task, of course, is not new. It has been a central hallmark of evangelical theology in every generation, and it continues to be universally acknowledged by contemporary evangelical theologians. In fact, acknowledgment of the Bible as our supreme authority for theological reflection forms the ongoing legacy of the Reformation within the evangelical tradition.

Some evangelical thinkers, however, take loyalty to the Bible to heights not intended by the Reformers and not in keeping with the broader tradition of the evangelical movement. In complex prolegomena to theology, they preface their systematic-theological construction with elaborate attempts to establish as the foundation for their labors the resourcefulness of the Bible. They argue for the divine nature of Scripture through a series of proofs, including appeals to externally verifiable "miracles," such as fulfilled prophecies, and internally focused discussions of the Bible's own claims about itself.

Yet all such attempts to establish the role of Scripture in theology, whether or not they are successful, are ultimately unnecessary. In engaging in the theological task, we may simply assume the authority of the Bible on the basis of the integral relation of theology to the faith community. Because the Bible is the universally acknowledged book of the Christian church, the biblical message functions as the central norm for the systematic articulation of the faith of that community. Consequently, the divine nature of Scripture or its status vis-à-vis revelation need not be demonstrated in the prolegomenon to theology. Sufficient for launching the systematic-theological enterprise is the nature of theology itself as reflection on community faith. And sufficient for the employment of the Bible in this task is its status as the book of the community.

The biblical documents mediate to the theologian the kerygma—the gospel proclamation of the early communities—which is likewise foundational to our exposition of the faith of the community. This kerygma is the primary norm for theology. For this reason, we acknowledge the biblical message as the first pillar on which the theologian constructs a theological model for the use of the church.

But theology is not merely the systematic repetition of the content of the Bible. As Karl Barth rightly declared, "Dogmatics as such does not ask what the apostles and prophets said but what we must say on the basis of the apostles and prophets."[15]

Although Barth's declaration is correct, standing alone it suffers from a glaring sin of omission. The theologian dare not immediately jump from listening to the apostles and prophets to speaking in the present context. Rather, the theological task demands that we look to an intermediate, mediating source that carries secondary importance: the theological heritage of the church.

Insofar as it is the product of the ongoing reflection of the church on the biblical message, this second norm for the theological enterprise is an extension of the first. In addition to mediating the kerygma, the gospel message, the narrative of God's salvific action toward humankind, the Bible provides the foundation for a corpus of basic Christian teaching that developed in the early church and has been transmitted from one generation of Christians to the next. The contemporary believing community continues in the tradition of those who give assent to this foundational doctrinal corpus. As a result, this body of beliefs likewise belongs to the faith of the church on which theology reflects. Robert Webber, who is one voice calling evangelicals to a renewed sympathy for the classical Christian creeds, asserts that this "content of Christian faith is basic to and even prior to theological formulation."[16]

But the assumption of an unaltered corpus of doctrine articulated for all time by the Christians of the early centuries, while in a sense true, nevertheless oversimplifies a complex phenomenon. All expressions of the faith, including the early creeds and all claimants to the status of being the eternal corpus of doctrine, are culturally conditioned. They were formulated in the linguistic and philosophical frameworks of the age in which they were written. Consequently, our understanding of the heritage of the church as a norm for theology must be nuanced.

The specific dimension of the heritage of the church useful to theology is the complicated and multidimensional flow of history as it describes the theological conclusions and solutions of the past. The church has continually sought to express its affirmation of faith in the context of the specific historical and cultural situations in which it has lived and witnessed to the revelation of God in Christ. The story of theological history, therefore, narrates the attempts by the believing community to explicate the meaning of the kerygma within these changing historical contexts.

The church's theological history is significant for theology today for several reasons. Past doctrinal statements and theological models are instructive for the present quest for a relevant theology. By presenting us with previous attempts to fulfill the ongoing theological mandate, they alert us to some of the pitfalls to avoid, and they suggest directions that might hold promise for our attempts to engage in the same calling in the present.

Theological history, therefore, serves as a reference point to us as we, like our forebears, seek to grapple with the meaning of the scriptural message and our loyalty to the triune God in the context in which we live as the people of God. Recent theological explorations have led to a growing acknowledgment among Protestants, including some evangelicals, of the importance of the heritage of the church in this dimension of the theological task. Many thinkers are now aware that we can read Scripture only in the light of hermeneutical history and the way the church employs the Bible. Consequently, we must engage in the theological discipline with an eye toward theological history. In the words of Clark Pinnock, "The positive role played by tradition is the guidance it gives us embodied in the distilled wisdom of the ages. . . . Tradition is a defense in the church against individualism in interpretation. . . . The church would be foolish to turn its back upon tradition."[17]

More important, however, certain past formulations have withstood the test of time. They constitute "classic" statements of theological truth. Thereby they stand as milestones in the theology of the universal church. These formulations, therefore, have a special ongoing significance in the church.

The special role of the classic theological formulations comes into clearer light when we remind ourselves of the broader historical implication of our act of confessing faith and consequently of our own theological statements. Throughout church history, Christians in each generation and each location have expressed faith in the one true God who has revealed himself in Jesus the Christ. In so doing, they have participated in the one church, the confessing church of all ages. In confessing faith today, therefore, we are but the contemporary embodiment of a legacy of faith that extends through time and encompasses believers of all ages. Hence our expression of faith is to be not only contemporary but also the confessing of the faith of the one people of God.

In the same way, we engage in the second-order task known as theology as members of a community of faith that spans the centuries. Because we remain participants in an enterprise that includes many generations, the theological heritage of the church is crucial to the formulation of our statements in the present. Our desire must be to remain within the one church of Jesus Christ. For this reason, contemporary theologians must take seriously the "universal doctrine" of the church in order to retain continuity with the entire body of the people of God. This "universal doctrine" is in part couched in the formulations that have withstood the test of time and have gained broad acknowledgment among Christians of many generations. This "universal doctrine" is likewise couched in the great theological literature of the centuries, which we therefore can read with great profit in the contemporary situation.

Past creeds and confessions of faith are not binding in and of themselves.[18] They must be tested by the Scriptures. Nevertheless, they are helpful as they provide insight into the content of the beliefs of the church and as they alert us to our own contextual presuppositions. Of course we must understand all such statements within their historical and philosophical contexts. It is the intent of a creed, not its specific wording, that is significant for contemporary theology.

In keeping with the ongoing concern for relevance, the contemporary context of the recipient of the kerygma functions as the tertiary pillar for theology. The theological task is to reflect on Christian faith commitment in the world in which the church seeks to live as the people of God. To fulfill this mandate, theologians must speak in a manner understandable to contemporary society, employing current thought-forms and addressing current worldviews. Likewise, if theology is to be truly systematic and meaningful, theologians must take into consideration the discoveries and insights of the various disciplines of human learning and seek to show the relevance of Christian faith for the human quest for truth.

In the theological enterprise the historical-cultural context of the faith community performs a crucial function.[19] The social community in which the people of God participate contains its own cognitive tools—language, symbols, myths and outlooks on the world—that facilitate identity formation and the experience of reality. If the faith community would address the gospel message to the aspirations of people, therefore, it must understand the identity-forming and experience-facilitating concepts of the society in which it ministers the confession "Jesus is Lord." The theologian seeks to assist the church in this mission by so understanding the cognitive framework of the surrounding culture that he or she can help fashion the church's message in accordance to the categories of the recipients.

In this task, the many current attempts to mediate the Christian faith confession to contemporary situations form helpful models. Contemporary theologians are at work developing theologies that can speak today. Their efforts are instructive for us as we join in this enterprise.

The history of theology indicates that the historical-cultural setting of the Christian community has always played a crucial role in its theological formulations. This influence has made and continues to make demands in several directions.

Although never the sole determining influence, the church's social-historical context presents specific theological issues with which the believing community must grapple if it is to speak a relevant message to the present. For example, broader societal questions and perceptions concerning the process of history and the goal of history influence theologians' interest in eschatology. This is not to suggest that the task of the church is merely to respond to society's latest moods. But it does indicate that at its best, theology seeks to respond to the perceived needs and questions posed by the surrounding society.

Not only does the historical-cultural setting play a role in determining the issues explored by theology, but it also functions in demarcating the ways theologians handle these issues. Repeatedly in theological history, the church has looked to the categories of society for the concepts in which to express the Christian understanding of its faith commitment. For example, when it set for all time the full deity and full humanity of Christ in response to the question of Jesus' relationship to God, the church chose Greek categories of ontology.

Likewise, theological explanations concerning the work of Christ have drawn from sociological and political realities of the surrounding culture.

Hence, as Anselm so keenly noted, the new feudalism of the early Middle Ages demanded a replacement of the older ransom theory of atonement (Christ was our ransom from the devil) to the newer satisfaction theory (Christ's death was a satisfaction offered for the honor of God, which had been offended by our sin). Later, when feudalism gave way to the era of national governments, the satisfaction theory was replaced by the penal-substitution understanding (which views Christ as paying the penalty due us as offenders of the divine law).

As these examples indicate, theologians have an ongoing task of listening to culture. Only by so doing are they able to construct theologies that can assist the church in formulating its message in a manner that can speak within the historical-social context.

But what is involved in this task of listening to culture?[20] According to Robert J. Schreiter, any attempt to understand a culture ought to be characterized by three concerns--holism, identity and social change. Our analysis of culture is holistic in that it seeks to include the broad diversity of that culture, rather than being reductionistic, concentrating on one part to the exclusion of others. The concern for identity means that our understanding is able to address the forces that shape identity in culture: what makes us who we are, and how we get that way. And any helpful analysis of culture must be able to deal with the dynamics of social change. To this end it listens for the dissonances that mark the advent or progress of such change.

Although all three characteristics cited by Schreiter are important, perhaps the second—the concern for identity formation—stands above the others. Above all, the message of the action of God in Christ is concerned with the creation of a new identity: the redeemed person participating in the redeemed society, enjoying community with all creation and with the Creator. In its attempt to articulate this message, theology must listen intently to the categories employed by a culture to express the universal human drive toward identity-in-community. As theologians we must continually ask: How does this culture understand the characteristics that give distinctiveness to a group? What bonds of commonality does the culture construct? And what are the processes by which a culture sustains such bonds?

As Schreiter notes, the cultural categories that express the drive toward identity "often center around two considerations: group-boundary formation and world-view formation."[21] Within any culture, the church constitutes a specific group with a specific worldview. Its task, however, is to be an inclusive people, to proclaim its worldview convictions in culturally understandable categories with the goal of expanding its boundaries to encompass all who come to embrace its fundamental loyalty to Jesus Christ. Theology facilitates this goal as it reflects on the Christian faith commitment in order to sharpen its relevancy for the contemporary setting.

In summary, then, en route to the fulfillment of its mandate a truly satisfying theology keeps its sources—biblical message, heritage and culture—in their proper balance. Although they can be discussed in isolation from each other, within the context of the theological enterprise these three norms are interrelated. The evangelical theologian must be an artisan who seeks to express the faith of the people of God by looking to the kerygma, the heritage of the church and the contemporary cultural situation of the faith community. Foundational to the fulfillment of our task as theologians is the message of the Bible mediated to us through the prophetic and apostolic testimony. In each generation, theology must be the articulation of the biblical faith. In our task, the common theological heritage of the Christian church likewise forms a guidepost. Hence, in the words of Robert Webber, "the means by which Christians hold their subjective interpretations in check, is the rule of universality, antiquity, and consensus."[22] But the articulation of the biblical faith in keeping with our theological heritage must always be directed toward the contemporary context. In setting forth our theological commitments, we look to culture as well. We employ the various cultural or philosophic forms of our world, so that the message of the Bible as passed on from generation to generation by the faith community may come to understanding in the present.

As we diligently draw these three sources into a creative, practical systematic theology, we fulfill the ideal set forth by John Calvin: "Our constant endeavor, day and night, is not just to transmit the tradition faithfully, but also to put it in a form we think will prove best."[23]

Sources and the Theological Landscape

The threefold source for theology outlined here suggests a specific criterion by means of which we may evaluate systematic theologies. Simply stated, we appraise theologies on the basis of their faithfulness to all three theological norms. Hence we may pose a three-part question to any theological proposal: To what extent does this theology articulate the biblical kerygma, reflect the faith of the one people of God, and speak to the contemporary historical-cultural situation in which the faith community seeks to proclaim the good news and live as the people of God?

The three-norm schema likewise is helpful in constructing a map of the landscape of the contemporary theological world. Despite the two-directional compartmentalization into "conservative" and "liberal" characteristic of many evangelical treatments of contemporary theology, the theological lay of the land, like any physical landscape, actually flows in three directions. So we may speak of three paradigm theological orientations, based on the tendency of theological movements to emphasize one of the three norms (often to the deprecation or loss—whether intentionally or inadvertently—of the others).

One basic theological orientation, which we can term *fundamentalism* or, better yet, *biblicism*, claims to embrace wholeheartedly the first pillar of the theological discipline, the message of the Bible. The chief concern of proponents of biblicism, understood in this context, is to remain faithful to the kerygma. So keen are these theologians to be biblical at all costs that they often meticulously employ biblically based terminology in their theologizing. Some even make a conscious attempt to use only the specific categories of the biblical authors themselves. Consequently, radical biblicists are suspicious of theologians who replace biblical categories with language drawn from other disciplines, including the modern sciences.

Whatever its faults, biblicism has one important caution for theologians. It serves as a reminder that fidelity to the biblical kerygma is nonnegotiable for any truly valid theology.

The biblicists' concern for fidelity to the Bible, however, disposes them to certain problems. Through their stringent utilization of biblical categories, biblicists run the risk of replacing systematic theology with biblical theology or of articulating the faith in language that is not understandable to the contemporary world.

It is surely correct, as biblicists sometimes claim, that in seeking to speak prophetically to the contemporary world, the church must declare the biblical message even at the risk of having its message rejected. But as messengers we must be sure that the stumbling-block in our proclamation is the "absurdity of the cross" and not the opaqueness of the categories we employ. In its quest to speak, the church must always formulate the biblical message in thought-forms that communicate with culture, with an awareness of the self-understanding of the culture to which we seek to minister. In fact, only by attempting to be heard by the world around us can the church truly come to grasp the biblical message, for that message is the good news of available salvation in the present and in the midst of the needs of contemporary people.

Not only does biblicism run the risk of not communicating with culture, but its mistrust of contemporary culture disposes it toward sectarianism. In the twentieth century, biblicist fundamentalists have upheld the principle of separation from theological liberalism. Unfortunately, this attitude has often degenerated into ecclesiological isolation as well, as in the name of separation fundamentalists have cut themselves off from valid expressions of the church—both historical and contemporary.

Often placed diametrically opposite to biblicism is a second theological orientation, which we may speak of as "progressivism" (sometimes designated in its radical form as "liberalism"). Progressives are committed to the tertiary theological norm, culture. Their goal therefore is quite different from that of biblicists. Progressives view the task of theology as that of presenting the Christian faith in terms the present culture can understand. To this end, they reinterpret biblical language in accordance with the language of the contemporary world or even replace biblical categories with terms reflecting current trends.

Progressivism offers an important reminder that theology by necessity must speak to culture; as theologians we must present the Christian commitment to Jesus in terms that are understandable to and meet the needs and aspirations of people today. But this legitimate concern of progressives can lead to an unmistakable loss of either the biblical witness or the heritage of the faith of the church.

In addition to biblicism and progressivism, there is a third but often overlooked current in theology. We may term this alternative "confessionalism" because its emphasis lies with the norm of heritage. The overriding concern of confessionalists is that theology remain faithful to the doctrinal tradition of the ecclesiological group to which they belong. Hence confessionalists tend to be loyal to the formulations of a particular church tradition (e.g., Roman Catholic, Eastern Orthodox, Lutheran, Wesleyan). Or confessionalists may appeal to a particular period of theological history (e.g., the patristic era or the Reformation). Likewise, confessionalists may elevate a particular doctrinal formulation (such as the Westminster Confession of Faith) or a particular theological program (e.g., dispensationalism, Calvinism or Arminianism), because they see these as foundational to the ecclesiological body to which they belong.

Confessionalists bear witness to the importance of the historical trajectory of the church. They call theologians to take seriously our place within the broader sweep of church or denominational history, or the heritage of a specific theological tradition, all of which are larger than the specific ruminations of any one contemporary thinker. Confessionalists likewise remind us that our task includes service to the church as a whole or to the specific expression of the church in which we participate.

Despite the crucial nature of the confessionalist concern, confessionalism runs the risk of growing deaf to the biblical critique of every confessional heritage or becoming irrelevant to the contemporary setting of the church.

This description of the theological landscape indicates that the term *conservative* may actually have several connotations. Most generally it is used to refer to those who are concerned to maintain fidelity to biblical doctrine (biblicists or fundamentalists). Yet *conservative* may be applied to those who elevate either of the other two theological norms as well. Confessionalists are conservative insofar as their interest lies in ensuring fidelity to the heritage of a specific confessional body. And "conservative liberal" is not a contradiction when used to refer to those who maintain loyalty to the cultural expressions of an era that in fact may have grown irrelevant or may no longer be understandable, or when loyalty to a specific cultural agenda places a theologian at odds with the other two theological sources. So evangelicals are not always wide of the mark when they accuse certain liberals of displaying a "fundamentalism of the left."

Rather than elevating one norm to the exclusion of the other two, the ideal theological model maintains a balance among all three concerns. A truly helpful theology must articulate the biblical kerygma, in a way understandable by contemporary culture, while maintaining a fundamental unity with the one people of God throughout history.

The Threefold Source and a Truly Evangelical Theology

Although it has often wandered from the goal, at its best the methodology of evangelical theology attempts to work toward the ideal of integrating the three norms of biblical kerygma, theological heritage and contemporary culture. In fact, we may define a truly evangelical theology as one that achieves the proper theological balance. It reflects the concerns of the three basic types of theology—biblicism, confessionalism and progressivism—for it builds upon the interplay of the three pillars of theology.

That a truly evangelical theology incorporates the first norm, the biblical kerygma, goes without question. The desire to take the Bible seriously as the book of the people of God has consistently been at the heart of the evangelical impulse throughout church history. More specifically, commitment to the biblical message—to the Spirit speaking through the Scriptures—as the final authority in all matters of faith and practice has been a hallmark of the broader evangelical tradition that appeals to the Reformation as its genesis. In fact, this commitment stands as one central contribution of evangelicalism to the church as a whole.

In addition to the centrality of biblical authority in the broader evangelical tradition, contemporary "card-carrying" evangelicals continue to set forth the concern for biblical theology and the defense of biblical doctrine inherited from the older fundamentalism out of which we emerged. As evangelicals we adamantly maintain that not only at its core but also at every juncture, systematic theology must remain true to the doctrine of the apostles and prophets and that biblical teaching must be applied to life as the standard for Christian conduct.

In addition to the emphasis on biblical authority, evangelical theology provides occasion for the attempt to remain faithful to the second pillar, the theological heritage of the church. Evangelicalism has always been conscious of its roots as a movement for orthodoxy and orthopraxy within and on behalf of the church as a whole. Throughout the movement's history, evangelicals have appealed to the early church, to the great thinkers of the patristic era such as Augustine, and even to certain medieval voices as providing the foundation and apologetic for the emphases of the movement. Evangelicals have always seen themselves as standing within the historic tradition of the one true church. In keeping with this consciousness of heritage, contemporary "card-carrying" evangelicals, following in the footsteps of the turn-of-the-century fundamentalists, repeatedly chastise their progressive opponents, claiming that their purported innovations run the risk of rejecting or forsaking what have been the teachings of the church throughout the centuries.

But above any other era since the apostolic, evangelicals elevate one expression of the heritage of the church: that of the Reformation. This "Reformation confessionalism" entails both a danger and an advantage. Attempted fidelity to the Reformation has meant that we have tended to find little of value in other traditions, specifically those of the Roman Catholic and Eastern Orthodox churches. The Roman Catholic Church has consistently been the object of evangelical polemic, which has served to keep alive the controversies of the sixteenth century. Even in the post-Vatican II situation some evangelicals have remained not merely distrustful of the Catholic Church but blatantly anti-Catholic.

There are signs of change, however. Charismatic evangelicals, for example, often enjoy fellowship with Catholic coexperientialists. Activist evangelicals repeatedly find themselves marching with Catholics on behalf of certain social causes, as has been evident, for example, in the antiabortion movement. And some noted evangelicals have left their denominations to find a new home in Roman Catholic or Orthodox churches.

While all evangelicals view the Reformation as of great consequence for theology today, there is diversity among us as to which aspect of the Reformation heritage ought to claim highest loyalty. As a result, there are Lutheran, Calvinist and Wesleyan evangelicals. And there are evangelicals who appeal to the free church tradition of the so-called Anabaptists of sixteenth-century Europe or to the radicals of English Puritanism who gave birth to the Baptists.

This diversity of heritage makes for diversity in thought within the agreed evangelical attempt to be broadly Reformational in outlook. The desire to build on the advances of the Reformation provides an important, positive opportunity for us as evangelical theologians. The interdenominational character of the movement can offer a broader perspective for the theological enterprise than what may be gained by remaining fixated on the heritage of a single denomination. Thus thinkers from diverse backgrounds—whether Baptist, Pentecostal or Presbyterian—have opportunity to learn from each other within a climate of fidelity to their own confessional heritage but also of mutual affirmation and respect. In this way we are spurred on to develop theologies that are denominational and yet reflect the broader heritage of the church as a whole.

Finally, evangelicalism provides a context in which to take seriously the pillar of culture. Evangelicals have tended to be more open to dialogue with contemporary culture than fundamentalists. In fact, many historians of these movements suggest that this open spirit, rather than doctrine (for the groups hold most points of doctrine in common), constitutes the most telling difference between contemporary evangelicalism and fundamentalism. Despite our openness, in this dialogue with culture we seek to remain cautious, lest the uniqueness of the gospel message be offered on the altar of the fashions of the day.

Critics to our right and to our left, however, are not always convinced that as North American evangelicals we are sufficiently cautious in approaching culture. The popularity and growth of evangelical churches, critics charge, have at times come in tandem with a cultural captivity to the American way of life and the policies of the United States government. This tendency has been augmented by the basically conservative theological orientation of evangelicalism, an orientation that easily spills over into political conservatism.

Among the vocal critics of evangelicalism on this point have been our Mennonite next-of-kin. C. Norman Kraus, for example, chastises the movement for its "accommodation to nationalistic American culture and its tacit espousal of nationalism and capitalism as *Christian* values." Kraus complains that "the movement has lacked a clear moral critique of American political and social policy based on a distinctively New Testament Christian ethic. In short, it has tended to reinforce capitalistic nationalism in the name of Christian moral values, harking back to a nineteenth-century 'Golden Age' when the evangelical social establishment dominated religion in the United States."[24]

The charge of Kraus and others is ironic, for evangelicals have long castigated the liberal tradition for its purported cultural captivity. Now the same charge is being directed at us. Even critics on the left are joining in the chorus, turning the tables on the evangelical critique of liberalism. Delwin Brown, for example, in a dialogue with an irenic evangelical takes the offensive against his opponent and the entire movement:

In other writings Clark Pinnock has characterized liberalism as the substance of modern culture wrapped in a thin Christian veneer. I do not accept that as a description of what I mean by liberal Christianity, but I do think it aptly characterizes much of today's evangelical movement. Far too much of modern evangelicalism is almost the purest form of "liberalism," in Pinnock's sense, that one could imagine. It is a modern ideology of class, race, or nation, or all three, sprinkled with splashes of a woefully diluted biblical witness.[25]

Clearly, evangelicalism is not exempt from the dangers that beset other expressions of Christianity. Hence, as evangelical theologians we must be vigilant lest our legitimate concern to speak *to* culture does not degenerate into merely an accommodation of the biblical message to the dictates *of* culture, thereby repeating the mistake of classical liberalism. Despite this ever-present danger, however, our commitment to biblical authority and our concern for fidelity to the historical faith of the church place us as evangelical thinkers, I believe, in the best possible position to avoid cultural captivity.

The revisioning of evangelical theology demands that we move beyond earlier evangelical theologians' focal interest in propositionalism without losing the central truth that approach embodies. To this end, we must revision the sources for theology. Rather than the focus on one theological norm typical of the classical expression of the coalition or the newer proposals that appeal to two or four sources, our revisioned theology must employ three norms: the biblical message, the theological heritage of the church, and the thought-forms and concerns of contemporary culture. Only in this way can our theology be at one and the same time, and in the best sense of these terms, biblicist, confessional and progressive.

But of these three sources for theology, throughout its history the evangelical movement has consistently sought to give primacy to the first norm, that of Scripture. To the question of the nature of biblical authority we now move.

5
REVISIONING BIBLICAL AUTHORITY

The older evangelical propositionalism captured a central truth, one we must retain in our revisioning of evangelical theology: the foundational belief that God has disclosed himself to humankind. Evangelicals boldly maintain that the primary focus of the divine self-disclosure is Jesus Christ and that the Bible is the deposit of the divine revelation in history. A revisioned evangelical theology, therefore, while seeking to be biblical, confessional and progressive, begins its enterprise with the Bible.

Without a doubt, the Bible is crucial to the evangelical project we share. Mark Noll correctly notes,

When examining the evangelical study of Scripture, everything hinges upon a recognition that the evangelical community considers the Bible the very Word of God. . . . Whatever else one may say about the Word of God (and many evangelicals are willing to recognize the supremacy of Christ as Word or to organize community life around the Word of proclamation), the Word of God always involves the Bible. Although evangelicals typically give some attention to the human character of the Bible, they believe that Scripture itself teaches that where the Bible speaks, God speaks.[1]

Many twentieth-century "card-carrying" evangelicals have sought to understand the evangelical commitment to biblical authority in terms of the word *inerrancy*. Regardless of the usefulness of this term, the recent emphasis on inerrancy is an indication that many thinkers construct the doctrine of Scripture with a view toward the divine nature of the Bible. The focus of their attention and the goal of their theological efforts is the demonstration that the Bible views itself as the Word of God. On the basis of this commitment to the Scriptures as divine they turn to engagement with the specific texts themselves.

As a result, many evangelicals take a cautious stance toward modern critical approaches to exegesis. Such caution is to some extent warranted, of course. But in seeking to defend the Bible from cavalier criticisms, we run the risk of taking a cavalier attitude toward the humanness that also characterizes the Bible. In our attempt to defend the Scriptures against their critics, we risk losing sight of the actual scandal that the Bible itself poses: that God addresses us through the instrumentality of human words. As G. C. Berkouwer insightfully says, "Our listening to God's voice does not need to be threatened by scientific research into Holy Scripture. Man's listening is only threatened when he stumbles over the *skandalon,* which in the Bible reaches, limits, and blesses us as the 'scandal' of Christ."[2]

To the extent that we seek to maintain the evangelical emphasis on the primacy of Scripture and the importance of approaching the Bible reverently and seriously, our intent in adhering to inerrancy is correct. However, while acknowledging the divine origin of Scripture, we can ill afford to overlook its human authorship. Consequently, our bibliology—our doctrine of Scripture—cannot merely be constructed "from above," that is, with a goal toward the establishment of its divine character as the first conclusion of theology. Instead it requires an equal movement "from below," a forthright acknowledgment that the divine Word in the Bible comes to us always and solely through human words, with the result that such human words are the Word of God (e.g., 1 Thess 2:13).

The articulation of a doctrine of Scripture that undergirds the creative tension between the divine and human in the Bible has been a grave challenge throughout church history. Dewey Beegle offers this sobering appraisal: "From Irenaeus in the second century up to the turn of the nineteenth century, the formulations of inspiration were essentially general affirmations of the divine and human aspects of Scripture. Nowhere were these two facets of the truth explicitly reconciled."[3]

Recent offerings, such as Clark Pinnock's *The Scripture Principle* (1984), are harbingers of a more conscientious attempt by evangelicals to give place to both the human and divine dimensions of the Bible. Nevertheless, the integration of the two remains an unfinished challenge. David Wright's appraisal is as perceptive today as it was in 1978: "We have to work out what it means to be faithful *at one and the same time* both to the doctrinal approach to Scripture as the Word of God *and* to the historical treatment of Scripture as the words of men."[4] But how can we keep the two in proper balance?

Scripture as the Source of Sustenance

A promising beginning point for the construction of an evangelical bibliology that acknowledges the Bible as simultaneously human words and the divine Word—that the Bible is God's Word to us in the form of human words—lies within the attitude many who belong to the wider circle of evangelicalism express toward the Scriptures. Evangelical spirituality views the Bible as the place—ultimately the only place—to go to find the words of everlasting life. As evangelicals we believe the Bible is, in Pinnock's description of this phenomenon, "the God-given documentation which preserves for all time the gospel of our salvation." Consequently, "ordinary believers know instinctively from the Spirit their teacher to go there to be nourished in their faith."[5]

Seeing the Bible as the source of spiritual sustenance is but the contemporary expression of the older Pietist tradition that has been an important molding influence within the broader evangelical movement. One crucial emphasis that characterized Continental Pietism dating to seventeenth- and eighteenth-century thinkers such as Spener and Francke was the importance of the spiritual condition of the reader: only the regenerate understand the Scriptures correctly.[6] For the Pietists, talk about the truth-claims of the Bible was less important than the fact that "truth claims"—that the Scriptures lay hold of the life of the reader and call that life into divine service.[7] For them, then, the ultimate goal of Bible study is the spiritual formation of the reader. Consequently, the Pietists could study the Bible both critically and devotionally. The Pietist way diligently brings one's hermeneutical skills to bear on a text, but then listens patiently to hear the voice of God speak through that text.[8]

This evangelical pietism resembles at certain points the approach to the Bible found in the Orthodox tradition. Orthodox thinkers also emphasize the importance of the spirituality of the reader and of obedient reading in the process of understanding the Bible. Mary Ford represents this view:

It is a commonplace among the Fathers of the Church that one must live the Gospel commandments in order to truly understand the Gospel. But when "hearing" is thought of as solely a conceptual understanding, then the holiness of the life of the interpreter, and his knowledge of spiritual realities, becomes irrelevant for interpretation. This is clearly not a Scriptural view, or one consonant with the Tradition of the Church. Rather, as we indicated, in Scripture, "hearing" is understood as a living out—as an experience which must precede real understanding. When this is grasped, we can see why the holiness of the text demands a holiness of the interpreter to make possible a full and proper interpretation.[9]

Similar to the German Pietists and in keeping with contemporary understandings of the hermeneutical process, Ford adds that this approach alone "enables an authentic understanding of the primary kind of knowledge which Scripture *intends* to communicate," namely, spiritual knowledge of God. She rejects the Enlightenment ideal of objective, neutral, presupposition-free reading. Instead, true understanding comes only to the person who approaches the text from within the context of the believing community, which alone provides the right presuppositions for the hermeneutical task.[10]

In taking this approach, both the spirituality of pietistic evangelicalism and that of the Orthodox tradition are merely embodying emphases of the biblical documents themselves. The writers repeatedly bear witness that the primary, central purpose of Scripture is to foster in us a relationship with God—that is, to advance the reign of God, which is the establishment of the redeemed community. The purpose of the Bible is to proclaim the good news of salvation to sinful humans and to mediate spiritual nourishment to believers. This biblical and evangelical spirituality carries several implications for our understanding of biblical authority.

Scripture and Spirit

The spirituality of evangelical believers suggests that our bibliology must revision the link between the Holy Spirit and Scripture. Several biblical texts speak of the Spirit as the wellspring of all life. As the Completer of the program of the triune God in the world, the Spirit not only creates life but is also the author of new life. The Spirit brings into reality the reconciled people of God, and he nourishes and sustains the spiritual life he creates. This means, however, that the purpose of Scripture is instrumental to the work of the Spirit.

The intimate relation between Spirit and Scripture is explicitly acknowledged in what Bernard Ramm calls the Protestant principle of authority: "The proper principle of authority within the Christian church must be . . . the Holy Spirit speaking in the Scriptures, which are the product of the Spirit's revelatory and inspiring action."[11] This position received its definitive articulation in the Westminster Confession of Faith: "The Supreme Judge, by which all controversies of religion are to be determined, and all decrees of counsels, opinions of ancient writers, doctrines of men, and private spirits, are to be examined, and in whose sentence we are to rest, can be no other than the Holy Spirit speaking in the Scripture."[12]

The source of our knowledge of divine truth is neither the Scriptures expounded according to our private interpretation alone nor any private, individual "word from the Spirit." Rather, it consists in an external principle—inspired Scripture—combined with an internal principle—the witness of the Holy Spirit. The Scriptures are the vehicle or instrumentality of the Holy Spirit through which he chooses to speak to the people of God.

A revisioned doctrine of Scripture must incorporate this insight concerning the integral relationship between the Bible and the Spirit.[13] Of course, this is not a recent discovery, but has been a central tenet of the evangelical tradition since the Reformation. Yet, rather than maintaining the proper relation between Spirit and Scripture, we have sometimes been guilty of rending the two asunder or collapsing the two together.

One of the least obvious means of dividing the Spirit from the Scriptures is latent in the theological methodology of Protestant systematic theology which separates bibliology from pneumatology. Consequently, the reestablishment of the integral link between Spirit and Scripture must begin methodologically through the reorientation of the doctrine of Scripture under the doctrine of the Holy Spirit.

The separation of the doctrine of Scripture from the doctrine of the Holy Spirit is evidenced in the classical Reformed approach. Many Reformed theologians treat bibliology as the central dimension of the discussion of revelation that is placed as prolegomenon to the development of systematic theology. The Bible is the deposit of special revelation. As a result, it supplies the foundation for the systematic theological enterprise, viewed as the systemizing of the doctrinal system deposited in the Bible. In this method, Reformed theology is simply mirroring the structure of the Reformed creeds. These generally, although not universally,[14] include a statement concerning Scripture as a separate article prior to the confessional statements concerning God. The Reformed approach seeks to carry out the theological task understood as the delineation of God's self-disclosure, and it elevates the Bible as the deposit of that divine revelation.

For these advantages, however, classical Reformed theology pays a price. Transformed in this manner into a book of doctrine, the Bible is easily robbed of its dynamic character. Separating the doctrine of Scripture from its natural embedding in the doctrine of the Holy Spirit conceptually separates Scripture from the Spirit, whose vehicle of operation it is. And treating revelation and Scripture as prolegomenon can easily result in a static understanding of the relationship between the two.

In contrast to the structuring of classical Protestant systematic theology and the Reformed confessions, the paradigm statement of faith of the ancient church, the Apostles' Creed, employs a simple trinitarian structure. There is wisdom in following the insight of the ancient structure in systematic theology. Its application to the doctrine of Scripture would place bibliology under the broader discussion of pneumatology, thereby considering the Bible as the book of the Spirit.

Delineating the doctrine of Scripture under the doctrine of the Holy Spirit has an added benefit. It facilitates a close connection of bibliology with ecclesiology and eschatology, both of which also fall under the broader rubric of pneumatology. The doctrine of the church reminds us that the Spirit is central to the life of the covenant people; eschatology reminds us that the Spirit is also God at work completing the divine plan. By understanding its connection to these dimensions of the Spirit's work, we can more readily see the Bible—the instrumentality of the Spirit—as the book of the community, the message of which is directed toward the "future," toward the goal, or telos, of the divine activity in history.

The reordering of bibliology under pneumatology is a natural extension of the classical evangelical acknowledgment of the twofold relationship between the Spirit and Scripture. The Holy Spirit, evangelicals confess, is the agent in both the original composition of the biblical documents (inspiration) and the ongoing understanding of the truth in those documents (illumination). However, our understanding of this twofold work of the Spirit toward the Bible is also in need of revisioning.

Inspiration and Illumination
Evangelical theology separates the Spirit and Scripture when it delineates bibliology as prolegomenon rather than as an aspect of pneumatology. In

another manner it readily collapses the two principles. This occurs chiefly through the traditional evangelical understanding of inspiration and illumination, which tends to focus on the former to the denigration of the latter.

Classical evangelical prolegomena generally move in a set sequence: revelation, inspiration, biblical authority, illumination.[15] Evangelical theologians begin with the affirmation that God has revealed himself. This self-disclosure has come through general revelation and more completely in special revelation.[16] The Holy Spirit preserved some of this special revelation by inspiring biblical writers to inscripturate it. The Bible, therefore, is God's Word. Because the Bible is the inspired Word of God, it is dependable, even inerrant. Consequently, it is authoritative. Finally, the Spirit now illumines the believer to understand its content.

Undertaken in this manner, the delineation of the doctrine of Scripture has as its goal establishing the divinity of the biblical writings as the Word of God. The theologian deduces this conclusion from a variety of considerations, including the Bible's own testimony, bolstered by evidences to its veracity in reporting facts that can be documented from history or science. The divine character of Scripture, in turn, forms the basis for the exegete's approach to the various texts, each of which shares in the status of the whole as the Word of God. What is important about the Bible, therefore, is first and foremost that it is inspired.

Despite its many advantages, the construction of bibliology in this manner, "from above" as it were, has certain shortcomings. It runs the risk of paying only lip service to the corollary affirmation that the biblical documents are human products. Although recent works of evangelical biblical scholars demonstrate an awareness of the humanness of the Bible, their theologian colleagues have not always kept pace. Rarely do our evangelical systematic theologies contain a well-articulated section on the Bible as a human book. For all our talk of "concursive action"—God and the human authors working together—when evangelicals do broach the topic of the human authors, we generally do so only to delineate how God providentially prepared his holy messengers to be vehicles for the inscripturation of special revelation.[17]

Thus, the traditional view defines inspiration in terms of the activity of the Holy Spirit in superintending the authors of Scripture in their writing. The older definition distinguishes an active sense (the action of the Spirit), a passive sense (the effect of the Spirit's action on the human author) and a terminal sense (the biblical writings as the deposit of what God desired to have written).[18]

In addition to the classical view's deemphasis of the human character of Scripture, it tends to deemphasize the Spirit's ongoing activity in speaking through Scripture in favor of a focus on the Spirit's completed work in inspiration. The doctrine of illumination is, of course, asserted in classical evangelical theology. Not only was the Spirit the moving force in the past action of inscripturating God's special revelation, but he assists readers to understand the meaning of the Bible today. Yet many evangelicals view illumination as only a secondary work, subservient to the primary matter of inspiration.

Pinnock states succinctly the popular evangelical understanding of the relation of illumination, as the Spirit's ongoing, secondary work, to the Bible, viewed as the product of the Spirit's primary, historical task in inspiration: "The Spirit works to bring each generation of believers as close to the Lord as the first apostles were and enables them to penetrate the same truth in relation to their different context. It is not that a new message will be given, but that the old message will continue to be made effective by the Spirit, as he helps us to reinterpret and apply the truth once delivered to meet new challenges."[19]

On the basis of an emphasis on the inspired nature of the Bible, the evangelical reader comes to the Bible with the purpose of delineating the revelatory message that was encoded in its pages centuries ago. This ancient yet eternal message is the "voice" of the Spirit. In this manner, we often collapse the Spirit into the Bible. We exchange the dynamic of the ongoing movement of the Spirit speaking to the community of God's people through the pages of the Bible for the book we hold in our hands.

As important as the emphases on the divine source and character of Scripture and on the finished work of inspiration are for a valid evangelical bibliology, we can no longer construct our doctrine of Scripture in the classical manner. The assertion of the inspiration of Scripture cannot function as the theological premise from which bibliology emerges, nor as the focal point of our understanding of the relation between the Spirit and Scripture. On the contrary, as the actual practice of evangelical spirituality suggests, the confession of the inspiration of the Bible is closely intertwined with the experience of illumination.

Inspiration is more closely bound to illumination than the classical evangelical description indicates. But how are we to understand this relationship? In recent years, this question has perplexed theologians from all Christian traditions. Their reflections have led to two broad, albeit not mutually exclusive, approaches in contemporary thought. Some thinkers move from the formation of the Scriptures as canon, whereas others emphasize the function of the Bible in the church.[20]

The canonical approach looks at the process of the formation of Scripture in an attempt to gain insight into the normativeness of the Bible for us today. It studies the origin, redaction and canonization of Scripture in order to uncover the paradigmatic pattern of interpretation and reinterpretation displayed in that process. The canonical understanding, which has gained adherents among evangelicals in recent years,[21] owes its impetus to mainline biblical scholars such as James Sanders and Brevard Childs.

Childs's interest lies with the ongoing authority that the traditions exercised in the life of the ancient community, which in turn finally led to the fixation of the biblical texts in their canonized form. The process is noticeable in Israel, for example, when the community recognized that the words of a prophet directed to a specific historical situation had authority apart from their original use. This authoritative tradition was ordered and transmitted in a form compatible with its function as Scripture for a subsequent generation, which form and use were likewise built into the structure of the text. The consequence then follows: "For this reason an adequate interpretation of the biblical text, both in terms of history and theology, depends on taking the canonical shape with great seriousness"[22]—that is, interpreting it in its canonized form and in relation to the ancient community of faith.[23]

For Childs, then, the historical-critical method of interpretation is inadequate to the complete hermeneutical task. It cannot raise "the full range of questions which the church is constrained to direct to its Scripture." Consequently, "when seen from the context of the canon both the question of what the text meant and what it means are inseparably linked and both belong to the task of the interpretation of the Bible as Scripture."[24]

Whatever his own intent may be, when viewed from within the context of evangelical concerns, Childs is calling for a closer link in our understanding between inspiration and illumination. The affirmation of biblical inspiration, he notes, is a statement of faith requiring no hidden apologetic. It is rather the claim that the Holy Spirit works through "the canonical context of the church."[25] Hence the development of the concept of canon was no arbitrary act, for thereby the church "bore witness to the effect that certain writings had on its faith and life."[26] The past experience of illumination, in other words, was intertwined with the affirmation of inspiration.

The functional approach moves in a somewhat opposite direction from the canonical. It starts with the role of the Scriptures within the Christian communities and then draws conclusions concerning the Bible's normative value.

The report to the 1971 Louvain meeting of the World Conference on Faith and Order, titled "The Authority of Scripture," offers a case in point. The document breaks with the older dogmatic tradition by not deducing the authority of the Bible from its inspiration. Instead, according to the characterization of Avery Dulles, "it establishes the authority of the Bible on the ground of its religious value for the church, and then proceeds to postulate inspiration as the source of that authority."[27]

The functionalist understanding is evident in the various attempts to speak of the Bible as the Christian "classic," including proposals of James Barr and David Tracy. It surfaces as well in the recent emphasis on narrative as a focal point for the theological enterprise. One proponent of this view is David Kelsey. In the church, he says, the Bible shapes new human identities and transforms both community and individual life.[28]

Neither the canonical nor the functional approach is without shortcomings and problems, of course. But in spite of these problems and despite the differences between the two approaches, their conclusion is similar. Both place inspiration and illumination close together, and both find the focus of the interrelation between the two aspects of the Spirit's work in connection with Scripture to rest with the believing community. The Bible now functions in the church as it functioned in the era of the fixing of the canon.

These recent attempts seek to deal with the nature of Scripture in a similar fashion. Simply stated, they declare that throughout history the people of God have confessed the inspiration of the texts now lodged in the biblical documents, because believers in every age hear in them the voice of the Spirit as they seek to struggle with the issues they face in their unique and ever-changing context. As in the past, so also today the Spirit chooses to speak through this human instrumentality. Consequently, we gladly affirm that the Bible is the deposit of divine revelation and readily acknowledge that these human words are the Word of God.

Advocates of this newer understanding run the entire gamut of denominational affiliation—Baptist, Presbyterian,[29] Roman Catholic.[30] Baptist New Testament scholar Edgar V. McKnight, for example, writes, "The Bible is seen, then, not as a finished and static fact or collection of facts to be analysed by increasingly sophisticated methods, but as a potentiality of meaning which is actualized by succeeding generations in light of their needs and by means of approaches supplied and authenticated by their worldviews."[31] And the newer awareness of the interconnection between the Spirit's enlivening of the texts and the confession of their authority as the product of God is not inimical to evangelicalism. On the contrary, it may actually be the point of the *locus classicus* for the evangelical doctrine of inspiration, 2 Timothy 3:16-17.[32]

Through the rare use of *theopneustos*, which perhaps intends an allusion to God's breathing into the nostrils of Adam and making him spring to life, the text declares that "God breathes into the Scripture," thereby making it useful. As the evangelical Greek scholar Edward Goodrick concludes, rather than supporting "the pristine character of the autographs," this text focuses on how valuable the Spirit-energized Scriptures are.[33] The church, in short, came to confess the inspiration of Scripture because they experienced through these writings the power and truth of the Spirit of God. These documents were, they knew, "animated with the Spirit of Christ."[34]

As we have noted, the reorientation of illumination and inspiration toward which a diversity of recent thinking is converging is closely bound up with a renewed understanding of the integral relation between Scripture and community. Because the connection between the Bible and the believing community is both historical and ongoing, it encompasses both illumination and inspiration.

The past relation between Scripture and the biblical people of God provides a more helpful understanding of how Scripture came into being than the classical evangelical view. In its discussions of inspiration, evangelical theologians tend to extend the model of single authorship to the composition of the Bible as a whole. Scripture, they assert, came to be as the Holy Spirit moved the individual authors to write their respective works. Although some of the canonical books were indeed written by individual authors (e.g., 2 Pet 1:20-21), the model simply does not fit all parts of the canon.[35]

In contrast to the understanding evangelicals often espouse, our Bible is the product of the community of faith that cradled it. The compiling of Scripture occurred within the context of the community. And the writings contained in the Bible represent the self-understanding of the community in which it developed. Or better stated, the Bible represents the understanding of those persons that came to form the enduring trajectory of that community, for at times the biblical writings offer a sharp critique of the attitudes and actions of the people as a whole.

The Scriptures witness to the fact that they are the final written deposit of a trajectory that incorporates a variety of elements, including oral traditions and other source documents. Within the community these took on, as it were, a life of their own, forming part of the authoritative materials that the community, under the direction of the Spirit in their midst, interpreted and reapplied to new situations. Through the moving of that Spirit, these materials were brought together at different stages in the life of the Old and New Testament peoples in response to perceived needs. All such needs, however, may be subsumed under the Spirit-produced sense of responsibility to preserve for the sake of the continuity of the community the record of or testimony to the historical events that shaped it, as well as the interpretation of these events and certain applications of them to community life.

From his review of the phenomena of the biblical documents, Paul Achtemeier concludes that "the major significance of the Bible is not that it is a book, but rather that it reflects the life of the community of Israel and the primitive church, as those communities sought to come to terms with the central reality that God was present with them in ways that regularly outran their ability to understand or cope."[36]

Our bibliology, therefore, must develop a deepened appreciation for the role of the community in the process that led to the composition, compilation and canonization of the Bible. Again Achtemeier's insights are helpful: "If it is true, therefore, that the church, by its production of Scripture, created materials which stood over it in judgment and admonition, it is also true that Scripture would not have existed save for the community and its faith out of which Scripture grew. That means that church and Scripture are joint effects of the working out of the event of Christ."[37]

This means that our confession of the moving of the Spirit in the Scripture-forming process, commonly known as inspiration, must be extended. It includes, of course, the writing of those several biblical books that came from the pens of single individuals. But it must also encompass the workings of God in the Hebrew and early Christian communities, insofar as these people participated in the process of bringing Scripture into being. By extension, the direction of the same Spirit in some sense blanketed the entire trajectory that climaxed with the coming together of the canon as the book of the people of God.

Critical to and lying behind the production of the biblical documents and the coming together of the Bible into a single canon was the illuminating work of the Spirit. The community found these books to be the vehicle through which God addressed them. But his illuminating task continues beyond the closing of the canon. Even now the Spirit attunes contemporary believers within the context of the faith community to understand Scripture and apply it to their situations.

In one sense, therefore, the contemporary illumination process resembles that experienced by the ancient communities. The Bible includes materials that represent how people within the community appropriated the oral traditions and writings of their heritage. But at the same time there remains one far-reaching difference. Israel and the early Christian communities engaged in the interpretive task within the context of the process of the formation of the canon. We now enjoy the illumination of the Spirit as he speaks to us through the completed Bible.

A clearer understanding of the ongoing role of the illumination of the Spirit in the formation of Scripture can lead not only to a more appropriate understanding of the process by which the Bible was formed but also to a deeper appreciation for the theological importance of the heritage of the Christian community. That heritage serves as a reference point to us as we grapple with the meaning of Scripture in the midst of the theological and ethical issues of our day.

One consequence of recent refinements in our understanding concerning the historical development of Scripture has been a movement toward convergence between ecumenical Protestants and Roman Catholics concerning the old question of tradition and Scripture. Avery Dulles reports that the way for this was paved by two significant meetings in the 1960s. Vatican II broke with the standard Catholic two-source theory, and the Montreal Conference on Faith and Order acknowledged the indispensability of tradition alongside the older principle of *sola scriptura.* [38] Against the former, scholars argue that Scripture and tradition are not "two distinct reservoirs, each containing a certain portion of revealed truth"; against the other, they observe that Scripture does not function alone, but "the Christian reads it within the church, in the light of the use the church makes of it." [39] Consequently Dulles concludes, "The documents of Vatican II and those of the Faith and Order Commission, while they do not totally overcome all the historic disputes between Catholics and Protestants, go a long way toward reconciliation. As a result, it is no longer safe to assume that either Protestants or Catholics adhere to the classical orthodoxies of their own churches, as expressed in past centuries."[40]

The renewed respect for the heritage of the church, or tradition, has not totally bypassed evangelicalism. Some evangelicals have set out on a path that led finally to Canterbury or even to Rome. Others, including certain free church evangelicals, have contented themselves with reassessing their own position. Pinnock, for example, acknowledges that "the positive role played by tradition is the guidance it gives us embodied in the distilled wisdom of the ages. In particular, it guards us against Scripture twisting. . . . Tradition is a defense in the church against individualism in interpretation. It is needed in order to protect God's people from private misinterpretations of the Bible. The church would be foolish to turn its back upon tradition."[41]

Beyond these and other benefits, a closer connection between inspiration and illumination would lead evangelicals to a more profound, Spirit-focused rather than text-focused understanding of the nature of biblical trustworthiness. Donald Bloesch has already pointed in this direction:

> When we speak of the trustworthiness of Scripture, do we not have in mind the trustworthiness of the Spirit who opens the eyes of the community of faith to the fullness of the meaning hidden in the text? The Spirit certainly does not impose completely new meanings on any given passage in question, but he manifestly draws out deeper meanings when the passage is seen in its wider context and is related to the existential situation of people today.[42]

In revisioning biblical authority, we would do well to build from this insight.

But would not the acknowledgment of a closer connection between the affirmation of inspiration and the experience of illumination expose us to the risk of subjectivism? Might it not tempt us to make the inspiration of the Bible dependent upon our hearing the voice of the Spirit in its pages, losing thereby the objective reality of inspiration? In short, is this not simply the older neo-orthodoxy dressed up in new garb?

The danger of subjectivism is indeed real, and therefore we must be cautious. Yet a lapse into this error is not inevitable. The focus on bibliology "from below" need not come at the expense of the corresponding bibliology "from above." Rather, we must continue to confess with the church that the Bible is objectively divine Scripture. It is Scripture regardless of whether we subjectively acknowledge it.

Nevertheless, the point remains: the bibliology "from above" cannot stand on its own, nor can the first thesis we make concerning the Bible focus on its divine nature. Both the historical development of Scripture and the ongoing piety of evangelicalism remind us that the acknowledgment of the divine character of Scripture is bound up with the work of the Spirit in illumination. As the community of faith hears the voice of the Holy Spirit in the pages of the Bible, it confesses that the Scriptures are the product of the inspiration of that same Holy Spirit.

The Task of the Spirit Speaking Through Scripture

A revisioned evangelical bibliology would forge again the relation between the Spirit and Scripture, which in turn would entail a more profound awareness of the interconnection between inspiration and illumination. But these emphases do not yet answer fully how the Spirit-illumined Scriptures function within the community of the people of God. The revisioned doctrine of Scripture, therefore, requires that we come to a more profound understanding of what the Holy Spirit accomplishes through Scripture, which is his instrumentality.

Foundational for an understanding of the ongoing activity of Scripture in the church is what Francis Schüssler Fiorenza calls its *constitutional role*. The Scriptures function as "the constitution of an ongoing community."[43] They hold this place insofar as they are the product of the foundational stage in the history of the church. In that they reflect the formation of the Christian identity at the beginning, they hold primary status at all stages in the life of the church as constitutive for the identity of the Christian community. They provide as it were the "ground floor" for the church, not simply because they came first but also because everything that follows is built on them.[44]

But how do the Scriptures become the constitution for us today? Evangelical spirituality has always seen the primary intent of the Bible in a manner that the emphasis on narrative has introduced only recently into mainline theology. Scripture is foundational in that it provides the categories for the Christian community.

The categories mediated to us through Scripture define and facilitate entrance into the faith community. Within the Bible is the story of God's work in the world, which begins at creation and climaxes in the eschaton. A crucial purpose of this story is to serve as the instrumentality of the Spirit in bringing sinful humans to change direction, to reinterpret their own narratives in terms of the categories of that story and to link their own stories with the story of God through connection with the story of the people of God. As we proclaim the "old, old story," the Holy Spirit calls its hearers into the family of God and assists them in viewing all of life from the perspective of that story.

The categories mediated to us in Scripture provide the paradigm for life within the church as well. These categories establish and preserve the identity of the community.[45] Through Scripture the Spirit works to shape our identity and existence as the community of Christ and as individual members of that people. As evangelical piety has always known, within the common life of the church the Holy Spirit employs the Scriptures, in the words of David Kelsey, "to nurture and reform the self-identity both of the community and of the individual persons who comprise it."[46] Hence Scripture is the bearer of a "life-changing" message, the good news of available power to live in newness of life, given to us by God in order that our hearts may be continually opened to receive the gift of the Spirit's energizing presence within.

To this end, the Bible orients our present both on the basis of the past and in accordance with a vision of the future. The past orientation transposes the contemporary hearer of the biblical narrative back to those primal events that originally constituted the community as a people. For the ancient Hebrews, the exodus was a central primal event. For the church the events surrounding the life, passion and resurrection of Jesus and the subsequent sending of the Holy Spirit are constitutive. But the goal of the narrative does not lie simply in the recounting of the story. Rather, through the retelling of the narrative, the Spirit re-creates the past within the present life of the community. And the texts thus provide paradigms and categories by means of which the community under the direction of the Spirit can come to understand and respond to the challenges of life in the present.[47]

William Herzog II summarizes the integration of past and present in this manner:

> In short, the living Word lures us into the world of the patriarchs and prophets or the times of the apostles and disciples not to leave us with their solutions but to model the perpetual task of the people of God who were called to interrogate their traditions and texts in the light of the living presence and activity of God so that we might catch a glimpse of *how* they entered faithfully into the creative work given to them. Seen in this light, Scripture reveals the task to which we are called, the fulfilment of which requires our creative participation.[48]

In addition to constructing our present from the past, however, the biblical story mediates a future orientation. The Bible declares God's intention for the world. It presents a vision of a ideal order in which human beings live in harmony with each other, with God and with the entire created order. James Barr's generalization may be too sweeping, but he is surely moving in the right direction when he notes, "Narratives are not necessarily written because of a primary interest in the past. They can be written to provide pictures of the promises of God which will come to pass in the future. Even if their literal purport concerns the past, their theological function and purpose may be directed towards the future."[49]

Like the orientation to the past, the future direction of the biblical materials seeks to impact our present existence. The Spirit employs the biblical vision to spur us to view our situation in the light of God's future and to open ourselves and our present to the power of that future, which is already at work among us and in our world.

In this entire process of ongoing dialogue, therefore, the Spirit is operative. From the primal question of our identity we move to questions concerning our vocation and how we are to think and live as members of the covenant community. Our ultimate quest, however, is directed toward the Spirit who moves us to ask the fundamental questions concerning life.

The considerations cited above suggest that the illumining work of the Spirit speaking through the Scriptures always occurs within a specific historical-cultural context. His activity during the biblical era which brought about the formation of the canon occurred within the changing contexts of the ancient Hebrew people and the early church. In the same way, the Spirit's illumination in the life of the church occurs within the various contexts in which the community of Christ exists.

The acknowledgment that the Spirit's illuminating activity occurs within the changing historical-cultural context of the people of God heightens our appreciation for the theological importance of cultural context in the hermeneutical task. We seek to listen to the voice of the Spirit through the Scriptures, and that voice speaks to us in the thought-forms, categories and conditions that impact our existence from the world in which we live.

The Bible as Revelation

But the burden of evangelicalism has always been to maintain that the Bible itself is revelation, the actual Word of God. A revisioned understanding of biblical authority, therefore, must take this concern seriously and delineate a proper understanding of the relation between Scripture and revelation.

The beginning point in this effort lies in what we have established thus far. As the evangelical bibliology asserts, the Bible is ultimately a function of the Spirit, for Scripture finds both its source and its abiding importance in the activity of the One who breathes it (2 Tim 3:16) and who breathes life into the community of its readers through the message proclaimed in its pages. This understanding of the Spirit's central role in forming Scripture and in applying the biblical message in the life of the community of faith suggests that pneumatology must function as the bridge between the concept of the historical revelation of God and the Bible as the instrument in our coming to know that revelation.

A twentieth-century thinker who pioneered a revisioned doctrine of Scripture was Karl Barth.[50] At the heart of the lasting vitality of this Swiss theologian's position are two theses he develops in the opening volume of his monumental *Church Dogmatics.*[51] The first thesis is Barth's conception of revelation as threefold. Primarily revelation is the Word of God disclosed, which is essentially Jesus the Christ, the Word incarnate. Secondarily revelation is the Bible as "the word of God written." And in a tertiary manner revelation is human proclamation of the word of God.

Barth's second thesis posits an intimate relationship among the three. The word written and the word proclaimed are revelation in a dependent manner, insofar as they are witnesses to God's self-disclosure. In short, for Barth the revelatory nature of the Bible is dependent on its function as a witness to the revelation of God in Jesus.

Although evangelicals may rightly resist what we find to be Barth's inordinate emphasis on the event character of revelation, he is surely correct in this delineation of the relationship between Scripture and Christ. As G. C. Berkouwer asserts, "Every word about the God-breathed character of Scripture is meaningless if Holy Scripture is not understood as the witness concerning Christ."[52]

The dependent relationship between the inscripturated word and the Word incarnate comes into focus through the scriptural concept of revelation. In the biblical documents "revelation" occurs primarily in the verb form and refers to the act of uncovering or unveiling what is hidden or veiled.[53] Only secondarily does it mean what is uncovered in the act, the static deposit produced by the revelatory action. Consequently, "the revelation of God" is the divine act of self-disclosure, which reveals nothing less than the essence of God, the ultimate truth which is God.

The fullness of the divine self-disclosure, of course, lies in the future at the eschaton. Revelation is nevertheless a present reality, for the eschatological unveiling of God has appeared proleptically in history. Central to the Christian faith is the confession that the focal point of this revelation is Jesus of Nazareth, "the Word made flesh." In relationship to Jesus and because of Jesus all history has revelatory significance, inasmuch as it derives its meaning from him. Understood from the perspective of the divine self-disclosure in Jesus, the events of history also provide insight into the nature of the God revealed in Christ. As Traugott Holz concludes in the *Exegetical Dictionary of the New Testament*, "According to the NT understanding, God reveals himself as he who acts in history. . . . And since, according to the NT, the decisive action of God occurs in the history of Jesus Christ, the word group clearly refers, in so far as it is used with reference to the actual event of revelation at all, to the *disclosure* of the reality of God as it is given with this history."[54]

In recent years, many evangelical thinkers have accepted the assertion widely held among neo-orthodox thinkers that God's historical revelation is mediated to us by means of act plus interpretation.[55] This understanding means that the focus of divine revelation does not lie in what we may call "brute historical facts" *(historie)* but rather in "interpreted facts" *(geschichte)*. Not an unexplained event but the interpreted event, within its place in the flow of events, is revelatory. Hence we encounter God through the interpreted story as it is retold and applied to life. In this encounter the Spirit, who empowers the interpreted story for the sake of our salvation, is present.

With this in view, we may approach the concept of "revelation" by appeal to the idea of "paradigmatic events."[56] A paradigmatic event is an occurrence that captures the imagination of a community to the extent that it shapes and forms its way of looking at the totality of reality and its understanding of its experience of reality. The community preserves the memory of the event, reinterprets the event in the light of the subsequent historical situations in which the community finds itself, and discovers in the event the source of an ongoing hope for the future. In this way paradigmatic events become a continual source of revelation, as each succeeding generation sees itself in terms of the events of the past history of the community.

The foregoing conclusions offer the way forward in our understanding of how the human words of the Bible are God's Word to us. In so doing they chart the way beyond the evangelical tendency to equate in a simple fashion the revelation of God with the Bible[57]—that is, to make a one-to-one correspondence between the words of the Bible and the very Word of God.

The typical evangelical understanding is unfortunate in that it fails to reflect the manner in which the New Testament authors use the phrase "the word of God." The evangelical scholar Paul Rainbow concludes from his textual study that the New Testament writers did not employ the phrase "the word of God" to refer to the Jewish Scriptures, as many evangelicals tend to do. Rather, they reserved the term for messages actually spoken by God to or through prophets and centering above all on the person and work of Jesus.[58] Consequently, according to the New Testament community, "the word of God" is the Holy Spirit announcing the good news about Jesus, which word the church speaks to us in the Spirit's power and by the Spirit's authority.

How does Scripture fit into this picture? Rainbow adds that because the Bible is a trustworthy record of God's speaking in the past, it provides "an absolutely sure criterion by which we can test the church's proclamation of the word of God in the present."[59]

Rainbow's conclusion, while perhaps revolutionary to many today, is not new among evangelicals. Its presence within our heritage is confirmed by Bloesch, who asserts, "A careful examination of early Protestant orthodoxy as well as of Puritanism and Pietism reveals that the distinction between the word of God and the words of the Bible was quite common."[60]

In an important sense, then, as Rainbow's thesis suggests, the "word of God," and hence revelation, precedes Scripture. Historically the divine initiation of communication from God to humankind went before the inscripturation process, and logically it carries priority. In this sense, the Bible presupposes the reality of revelation.[61] "The Bible is a divinely appointed channel, a mirror, or a visible sign of revelation," to use the words of Bloesch, who claims that this and not the characterization of fundamentalism was the position of the church from the patristic era through the Reformation.[62]

In another sense, however, revelation and Scripture are interrelated. The divine self-disclosure did not occur at once, prior to its inscripturation, but rather arose together with the process of the development of canonical Scripture. God's revelatory work came in part in and through the formation of Scripture, as the community of faith under the guiding hand of the Spirit struggled with the ongoing work of God in the world in the context of the earlier divine self-disclosure and the Scripture traditions that the earlier events called forth.

For example, the early Christians faced squarely the challenge to the heritage of monotheism posed by their foundational confession of Jesus' lordship and the undeniable experience of the presence among them of the Holy Spirit. The final outworking of their reflection was the doctrine of the Trinity.

God's revelatory work included as well the community's wrestling with the implications of the divine self-disclosure for life. God had entered into covenant with them, and because he is a holy God they were called to be holy as well. The Bible provides insight into the process by which the biblical people, under the guidance of the Spirit, came to discover the practical implications of the divine holiness for their own vocation as God's covenant partners.

God's ultimate self-disclosure, however, lies yet in the future. Consequently, even after the closing of the canon the church participates in the ongoing challenge of exploring the outworking for faith and life of its calling as the community of Christ.

Yet intervening events have introduced one crucial difference. The church now seeks to be the faithful people of God with completed canon in hand. We do not share in the task of Scripture formation. Rather, we seek to be the continuation or contemporary expression of the people whose identity and existence, because it is bound to the God who has disclosed himself in history, is consequently bound also to the Bible.

The discovery that the Bible in some sense presupposes revelation indicates that at least from our perspective Scripture is servant to revelation,[63] just as it is servant to the work of the Spirit. This is to say that the Spirit-energized message presented through Scripture takes primacy over the vehicle by means of which it is transmitted. The subservient character of the Bible to both revelation and the Spirit forms the context in which to set forth the authority of the Bible.

On the basis of this understanding of revelation, we may term the Spirit-illumined Bible "the revelation of God." The Bible is God's word to us. The connection between the Scriptures and revelation is threefold.

First, the Scriptures are revelation in a derivative sense. The Bible is revelation because it is the witness to and the record of the historical revelation of God. It testifies that God has indeed revealed himself. God has, as it were, lifted the veil. No longer is God hidden; God now stands for all time as the Revealed One. God has revealed himself and his intentions for creation in historical events prophetically interpreted and applied to life. The Bible is the written testimony to and deposit of this divine self-disclosure. In the Bible we read the historical events and their interpretation, for the Scriptures faithfully transmit interpreted salvation history to the contemporary reader.

In this sense, the Bible is divine truth. In fact, there is no other book to which we can go in order to learn about God's action in history to disclose himself to humankind. There is no other valid message about God but the biblical message. In this sense the Bible is God's word to us.

Second, the Bible is revelation in a functional sense: it is revelatory. Scripture points beyond itself, directing the reader's attention to the revealed God and informing the reader as to how God can be known. In fact, the message of the Bible is the instrumentality of the Spirit in authoring salvation and sanctification in us. As the Spirit illumines our hearts to understand and respond to the scriptural texts that he brought into existence, these human words—which always remain objectively the word of God in the sense noted above—become the word of God in our subjective experience.

Consequently, we must not idolize the Bible itself, as some nonevangelicals accuse us of doing.[64] Scripture is not an end in itself. Rather, we honor, and ought to honor, the Bible as the Spirit-inspired and Spirit-illumined means to knowing God. There is no other way of coming to know the divine reality except through an encounter with the living God. And this encounter is facilitated by the biblical message. In this sense the Bible is God's word to us.

Third, the Bible is revelation in the sense of an intermediary. It mediates to the reader the proper understanding of what God is like. It is God's word to us in that it is the word about God.

Ultimately, the subject matter of all Scripture is the triune God, whose nature is portrayed therein as love and who is described in its pages as the Savior God. The Bible portrays the outworking of God's character through the story of God's activity in history in bringing about salvation. As the Spirit illumines our hearts to grasp the biblical message, we come to understand God as loving Savior. As it mediates this awareness to us, this book is God's revelation. In fact, there is no other source to which we can turn in order to read about the character of God. In this sense the Bible is God's word to humankind.

Because the Bible is revelation in this threefold sense, the Spirit speaking through its pages is our sole authority. Only the Bible is so intimately related to the historical revelation of God as itself to be termed "revelation." Only the Bible constitutes the written record of the central revelatory historical events, together with the prophetic interpretation and application of these events. Only the Bible directs our attention to God in Christ, thereby bringing us face to face with the loving Savior God. As John Baillie writes, "The Scriptures are holy because they are the vehicle through which the Gospel is communicated to us."[65]

Properly understood, biblical authority must be affirmed as wide in scope, even all-encompassing for our lives as believers. Evangelicals are in basic agreement that the biblical writers claim authority in what we often call "matters of faith and practice." The Bible's authoritative status radiates outward from any narrow conception of this phrase, however, until it encompasses all of life. This phenomenon is a function of the all-encompassing nature of religious conviction.

Try as we will, we cannot successfully marginalize our religious orientation to the fringes of life, for religious commitments ultimately affect all areas of personal and corporate existence. This means, however, that whatever is determinative of these convictions will become the ultimate authority over our entire being. Consequently, to confess that the Bible is authoritative for "faith and practice" means that the Scriptures will permeate all of life. Placing ourselves under the teaching of the Bible commits us to confessing a biblical worldview. And a biblically informed outlook toward the world will eventually permeate our attitudes and outlooks toward every facet of life. The acknowledgment of biblical authority in faith and practice demands, therefore, that we apply to every area of life what the Spirit is speaking through the Scriptures, just as Jesus admonished his hearers to put into practice his sayings (Mt 7:24-27), an admonition echoed by James' entreaty that we be "doers" and not only "hearers" of the Word (Jas 1:22-25).

The Bible therefore may not be the kind of authority on the various branches of modern learning that many believers might want to maintain. Nevertheless, in a more profound sense its authority extends to every dimension of the Christian's outlook. H. N. Ridderbos summarizes this interesting relation:

> God speaks to us through the Scriptures not in order to make us scholars, but to make us Christians. To be sure, to make us Christians in our science, too, but not in such a way as to make human science superfluous or to teach us in a supernatural way all sorts of things that could and would otherwise be learned by scientific training and research.
>
> What Scripture does intend is to place us as humans in a right position to God, even in our scientific studies and efforts. Scripture is not concerned only with persons' *religious* needs in a pietistic or existentialist sense of that word. On the contrary, its purpose and authority is that it teaches us to understand everything *sub specie Dei*—humanity, the world, nature, history, their origin and their destination, their past and their future. Therefore the Bible is not only the book of conversion but also the book of history and the book of creation. But it is the book of history of salvation; and it is this point of view that represents and defines the authority of Scripture.[66]

This takes us back to the point at which we began. The evangelical commitment to the Bible is crucial, for Scripture forms the foundation for the evangelical ethos. If at the heart of evangelicalism lies our common vision of the nature of being Christian and if this vision is linked to the nature of the stories of our "experience with the Lord," then the Bible is significant. The Scriptures provide the categories by which we can understand ourselves and organize our narratives. And they determine what constitutes presence within the community of the faithful followers of the God who is revealed in Jesus Christ.

In short, from the message of the Bible we gain our identity as the people of God. And through the Bible we learn what it means to be the community of faith in the world.

6
REVISIONING THEOLOGY'S INTEGRATIVE MOTIF

I n addition to employing proper sources—the biblical message, the theological heritage of the church and the thought-forms of contemporary culture—a helpful theology incorporates what may be called a proper "integrative motif." Theology's integrative motif is that concept which serves as the central organizational feature of the system, that theme around which the systematic theology is structured. Such a motif is integrative, in that because of its location at the heart of the theological system it focuses the issues discussed and illumines the formulations of our responses to these issues. We may term this integrative motif the "orienting concept," for it provides the thematic perspective in light of which all other theological concepts are understood and given their relative meaning or value.[1]

Theological history has witnessed the devising of many integrative motifs. The great systematizer of the medieval church, Thomas Aquinas, for example, constructed his theology around the concept of the vision of God. The highest human activity, he maintained, is the intellectual contemplation of the divine substance. His theology was an attempt to assist in this pursuit, both in this life and in the next.

While Martin Luther never wrote a systematic theology in the usual understanding of that term, his works nevertheless reveal an integrative motif central to his thinking—justification by faith. Luther's theology proclaimed that the fundamental human quest for right standing before God finds its answer in the divine declaration of righteousness bestowed by grace on the sinner who receives God's provision by faith.

The other seminal theologian of the Reformation, John Calvin, focused his theological work on the theme of the glory of God. All of history and, in the end, eternity itself are the outworking of the decision God made before the creation of the world, according to Calvin. This divine decision, in turn, directs all events to the glorification of God.

Other examples of theologians who oriented their thought around an integrative motif could be added. John Wesley was captivated by the idea of grace, or perhaps better stated, responsible grace.[2] Friedrich Schleiermacher worked from human religious experience. And Karl Barth centered on the nature of revelation, the self-disclosure of the triune God to the human person.

Currently several themes are being presented as possible integrative motifs for theology. Certain fundamentalists and evangelicals look to the dispensations of salvation history[3] or to the doctrine of Scripture[4] as their unifying theological theme. In progressive theological circles, the process philosophy of Whitehead is influential as an integrating concept for theology.[5] One of the most widely employed themes in recent decades has been liberation. Originating within black theology in America[6] and in Latin American liberation theology,[7] its use has spread to thinkers in other groups as well. A related movement, feminist theology, utilizes the experience of women as the organizing principle for theological reflection.[8]

More recently, narrative theology, which emphasizes personal histories and the Bible as story, has gained attention, even among evangelicals.[9]

But none of these themes has been as widely employed in the twentieth century, whether in mainline theology or within evangelicalism, as the concept of the kingdom of God. Consequently, when we ask what theme can best serve as the integrative motif for a revisioned evangelical theology, we must look first to the idea of the kingdom or the reign of God. So our first question is, To what extent and in what form does this theme hold promise as a continuing focal point for theology?

The Kingdom of God as a Theological Motif

Already before the advent of the twentieth century the concept of the kingdom of God began its dominance as the central theme of theological discourse, not only among evangelicals but also in the wider theological arena. But with the coming of the twentieth century, the theme of the kingdom received renewed interest and a new thrust in both New Testament studies and systematic theology.[10] The influence of the concept has been both direct and indirect. It has been directly influential in theology insofar as it has formed the integrating motif for several theological proposals. But beyond its use as an explicit central theme, the idea has provided the foundation for various contemporary theological movements, including the theology of hope and liberation theology. In fact, at least until recently, it could have safely been said that the story of twentieth-century theology has been the story of the development of theologies of the kingdom of God.

But how are we to understand the concept of the divine reign or the kingdom of God? Despite the term's widespread use, its correct meaning has been the subject of intense debate in both New Testament studies and systematic theology throughout the twentieth century. This discussion forms an important background for the potential use of the kingdom theme as an integrative motif for evangelical theology.

The twentieth-century debate concerning the nature of the kingdom of God originally arose as a reaction to the use of the motif in classical Prot-

estant liberalism. Thinking in the previous century built from the work of
the "father of modern theology," Friedrich Schleiermacher. The focus of
Schleiermacher's inquiry was his assertion that religion primarily has to do
with what he called "God-consciousness." Because Jesus enjoyed a full God-
consciousness, Schleiermacher argued, he is able to bring us into a vital
relationship with God. This shared God-consciousness, in turn, marks us
as a society of the followers of Jesus, the church, which for Schleiermacher
is closely connected to the kingdom of God.

Subsequent thinkers built on Schleiermacher's linkage of the kingdom
of God with the society of believers. Albrecht Ritschl, for example, developed the ethical concept of the kingdom of God implicit in Schleiermacher's thinking. Ritschl understood the kingdom proclaimed by Jesus to refer
to the unity of humankind organized according to love.[11] Christian faith
grasps this kingdom revealed in Christ as the highest good and goal not
only of humanity but also of God himself.[12] In this manner Ritschl iden-
tified God's being with the progress of the kingdom of God in the world.

Ritschl's program was incorporated into the thinking of Adolf von Harnack. According to Harnack, throughout the history of the church the
gospel has been overlaid with husks of alien philosophical concepts, such
as the Greek identification of the Logos with Christ.[13] Nevertheless, he
added, the gospel has survived wherever Jesus' pure and simple message
of the kingdom of God has been accepted as the highest and most glorious
ideal known to humankind. This ideal is "the prospect of a union among
men, which is held together not by any legal ordinance, but by the rule of
love, and where a man conquers his enemy by gentleness."[14]

The apex of the liberal understanding of the kingdom came in the social
gospel movement. Proponents of the social gospel denied that Jesus understood the kingdom of God as either the realm of the afterlife or a future
perfect order subsequent to his Second Coming. Rather, for him it is an
earthly society in which all humans live together in cooperation, love and
justice. In keeping with this understanding, social gospelers sought to coop-
erate with God in the construction of the ideal society.[15]

The goals of the social gospel were aptly articulated by an early architect of the movement, Walter Rauschenbusch. His books outlined the applications to concrete social life of the ethical aims and ideals of the kingdom of God, understood in the social gospel sense. In *Christianity and the Social Crisis* (1907), for example, he asserted that being a Christian in the present social crisis meant working for the salvation (reform) of economic structures that perpetuate poverty. Exemplifying the central themes of the social gospel, he declared that the essential Christian task is "to transform human society into the Kingdom of God by regenerating all human relations and reconciling them in accordance with the will of God."[16] He specifically singled out laissez-faire capitalism as a part of the kingdom of evil and called on Christians to lead a new revival, in which not only individual souls but entire corporate entities and social structures would repent and be saved. Later, in *Christianizing the Social Order* (1912), Rauschenbusch offered specific suggestions for the revival he envisioned—the progressive approximation of the kingdom of God in human society. And in what became the systematic theology for the movement, *A Theology for the Social Gospel* (1917), he attempted to redefine every major Christian doctrine in terms of the central unifying theme of the kingdom of God.

But even as Rauschenbusch was delineating the implications of the liberal understanding of the kingdom of God, its theoretical foundations were being eroded by the rediscovery of the apocalyptic element in the Bible. As scholars began to see that the apocalyptic vision of the world was a central feature of the New Testament writings, they came to the parallel realization that the biblical portrait of the kingdom was not that of an ethical human society of people of good will founded by Jesus. Instead, the biblical documents speak of a catastrophic act of God breaking into history.

The initial impetus for this far-reaching shift in understanding came in a little book, *Jesus' Proclamation of the Kingdom of God* (1892), written by a son-in-law of Albrecht Ritschl, Johannes Weiss. From his study of the authentic sayings of Jesus, Weiss concluded that in Jesus' mind the kingdom was wholly future (hence the designation of Weiss's position as "consistent eschatology"). Further, Weiss asserted that Jesus did not conceptualize the kingdom as a society he would establish, but as an eschatological in-breaking of God into history. Consequently, Jesus stood in the ancient apocalyptic tradition, not the tradition of the liberal ethical moralists of nineteenth-century Europe.

Weiss asserted that Jesus never equated the kingdom with the society of his disciples or the larger fellowship of those who follow him. In fact, Jesus rebuked all who actively sought to bring in the kingdom rather than patiently waiting for its arrival (Mt 11:12). Further, the mystery parables of Matthew 13 refer not to a growing society of persons, but to the fact that "an obstructed and seemingly unsuccessful preaching will at last, through God's intervention, have its reward and result."[17] Jesus' own prayer "Thy kingdom come" was to Weiss further confirmation that in the Lord's understanding God's rule was yet future and would come according to God's prerogative.

From these considerations, Weiss asserted that there were three aspects of Jesus' understanding of his mission. First, he viewed himself as the bearer of the Spirit of God against the kingdom of Satan, the one entrusted with the task of driving the present world ruler from his position of lordship. Second, Jesus saw his mission as proclaimer of the gospel message of the kingdom: God would establish his kingdom; therefore, people must prepare themselves for its arrival. When Jesus' hearers failed to show fruits of repentance, and when their leaders blasphemed the Spirit, Jesus added a third aspect: he must die in order to remove the guilt of the people. At death he would be installed in heaven, and his disciples would continue his proclamation of the kingdom message, resulting in repentance on the part of their generation. Consequently, Jesus refocused his immediate task toward the gathering of a band of followers who would await the kingdom of God.

During the first half of the twentieth century an alternative to Weiss's understanding of Jesus' view of the kingdom emerged. A leading proponent of what has come to be known as "realized eschatology" was the British scholar C. H. Dodd. Dodd denied that Jesus was merely the herald of the kingdom of God who waited for its coming. Rather, Jesus was the inaugurator of that kingdom, who saw in the events surrounding him indication that "the sovereign power of God has come into effective operation."[18] Therefore Jesus' message was not that a kingdom would come in the future, but that through his ministry the eschatological events were now transpiring. The thrust of the entire New Testament, Dodd added, reflects this. The biblical authors were convinced that the eschatological hopes of the Old Testament had all been fulfilled in Jesus. God's formerly hidden rule was now revealed. Evil had been overthrown, sin had been judged, and new life was available for God's people.

Obviously, consistent eschatology and realized eschatology differed with each other concerning the time of the kingdom. But their differences extended as well to the question of its nature. Consistent eschatology emphasized a temporal dualism: the kingdom is a historical event that ends this age and begins a new chapter in world history. Realized eschatology, in contrast, posited an existential dualism: the kingdom is a sphere of existence into which the disciple enters now.

By the middle of the century, the debate between Weiss and Dodd was resolved through a third, mediating position. Although differences of opinion remained as to how the two dimensions fit together, New Testament scholars came to agree that in Jesus' mind the kingdom of God was both present and future—already and not yet—and it was both an event and a sphere of existence.

Systematicians employed the findings of their New Testament colleagues to develop a kingdom theology. This theology claimed that Jesus himself had inaugurated this kingdom through his proclamation of the rulership of God, his decisive battle against the forces of evil and his provision of reconciliation and life for human beings. Yet the consummation of the reign of God remains future, it added. The power of the "age to come" has broken into history and is therefore present, but we will not experience its fullness until the end of the age.

These developments in the wider theological world found their parallels within evangelicalism. The twentieth century witnessed the increased influence of dispensationalism, with its orientation to a future, millennial kingdom. After midcentury, however, the already/not yet consensus was introduced into conservative circles by the Fuller Seminary New Testament scholar George Eldon Ladd. Perhaps in part owing to Ladd's influence, evangelical thinkers of differing millennial persuasions have converged on a viewpoint similar to the position he so eloquently set forth. Hence both amillennialist[19] and dispensationalist[20] scholars now speak of the kingdom as both present and future.[21]

In recent years, the older consensus has begun to give way to a newer understanding that has deepened the insights of the already/not yet view.[22] Certain thinkers now argue that the phrase "the kingdom of God" points to the self-disclosure of God, "God in strength"[23] or the sovereign activity of God.[24] It is the ultimate intervention of God in human affairs. The coming of the kingdom, consequently, creates a new way of life in the present.

What can we conclude from the debates of the twentieth century concerning the kingdom of God? On the one hand, the divine reign is related to Christ's first advent. In a sense it is a reality that people can enter (Mk 9:47; Mt 21:31-32). It is the kingly power of God.[25] Hence the kingdom is a "sphere of existence" in which people are called to live. It is an incorporation into God's powerful invasion of our world; as such it consists in doing the will of God (Mt 6:10; 7:21-23) and demands a radical decision (Mt 13:44-46). To enter the kingdom means to participate in "the already inaugurated explosion of God's power into the world."[26] On the other hand, the consummation of the divine reign awaits the glory surrounding Christ's second advent. One day all creation will be brought into conformity with the divine intent. Only then will the kingdoms of this world truly become the kingdom of God and God's will truly be done on earth as it is in heaven.

As this survey of the discussion suggests, scholars have found much to commend the use of the concept of the kingdom of God as a central motif in theology. The usefulness of the theme has made it a widely employed concept in contemporary theology[27] (although it has come under some attack as being unreconcilable with feminist concerns[28]).

The theological employment of the theme of God's kingdom is not confined to the modern era. Throughout its history the church has pressed the concept into service to express its understanding of the significance of Christian faith. Its popularity is not hard to understand, for the kingdom of God is a central biblical theme. In the representation of Jesus' ministry found in the Synoptic Gospels the kingdom of God plays an obvious central role. This same theme, while not as pronounced, is developed in the Old Testament and utilized elsewhere in the New Testament as well.

But exactly how do the biblical writers use this concept? What do they mean by "the kingdom of God"?

As we would expect, Jesus' use of the term "the kingdom of God" arises out of an Old Testament context. The Hebrew root is found in the verb *mālak* ("to be king," "to rule"). Of the several cognates of this term, three are most important. *Mᶜlûkâh* generally refers to "kingship" or "royalty"— that is, a quality of rulership. On several occasions, however, it carries a second meaning, the aspect of physical "realm." The psalmist declares that God possesses a universal right to rule (Ps 22:28). The prophet Obadiah looked for the day when God would reign in Israel (Obad 21).

A second cognate, *malᶜkût*, means primarily "royal honor," "power," "dominion" or "dignity," but it is also used to refer to a king's reign, or even to the realm ruled. In fact, *malᶜkût* undergoes an interesting development from the early to the late Old Testament books. In the earlier works the term is less common and generally refers to the kingship of a monarch. In the late books this usage is maintained, but to it is added the concept of "realm." The term is used in conjunction with "Yahweh" to declare that God's dominion is universal (Ps 103:19) and everlasting (Ps 145:13).

By far the most frequently used cognate of *mālak* is *mamlākāh*. Like the others, it carries two basic meanings, "kingdom" (i.e., "realm") and "sovereignty" (i.e., "right to rule"). It is also used with reference to Yahweh. David acknowledged that God's right to rule is universal (1 Chron 29:11). Elsewhere, Abijah claimed that even the northern ten tribes lay under God's kingship (2 Chron 13:8).

This short word study suggests three conclusions. First, in the Old Testament no great distinction is made between the concept of a monarch's right to rule and that of the physical realm of the king's dominion, for these are two poles of one basic concept. Second, the Old Testament declares God's right to rule as properly extending over the entire world, even though not all human beings acknowledge this right. Third, Israel is God's kingdom in a special way, in that Israel acknowledges God's kingship. Yet one day all nations will follow Israel in this confession.

The New Testament understanding of God's kingdom follows closely that set forth by the Old. The vast majority of occurrences of the Greek word *basilea* are found in the Synoptics. The first three Gospels reveal the same basic tendency as is present in the Old Testament. Jesus sometimes suggests that the kingdom is a present reality (Lk 17:20), present because the prophetic time is fulfilled (Mt 11:2-56; Mk 1:14-15; Lk 4:21) and Satan has been defeated (Mt 12:28-29; Lk 10:9, 18). But Jesus also declares the kingdom to be future (Lk 21:31); this future reality is nevertheless at hand (Mk 1:14-15). As to Jesus' understanding of the nature of the kingdom of God, it is both a realm over which God rules and also God's reign, rulership, or right to rule.

Elsewhere, the New Testament documents indicate the same marked patterns of usage. The aspect of temporality is variously addressed. The kingdom is sometimes seen as present, sometimes as future. The same is true concerning the nature of the kingdom. Sometimes emphasis is given to the kingdom as a realm ruled, whereas other times the rule or the rulership of God is in view.

Helpful to a theological understanding of the concept of the kingdom is a differentiation between the de jure (in principle) and de facto (in fact) sovereignty of God. As Creator, God is de jure monarch; that is, the kingship belongs to God by right. Because God created everything, God possesses the right to rule over all creation. In the same way the entire universe is the kingdom of God—the realm of God's dominion—de jure. In principle all that is constitutes the realm over which God's kingship is exercised.

What is true de jure, however, is not yet fully true de facto. Humans have been given the privilege of acknowledging God's rule, but have rejected it and formed a rebellious enclave. Another asserts a claim to be king in this sphere. As a creature and not the Creator, this de facto ruler is a usurper who does not possess the inherent right to rule that is God's alone.

Jesus came bearing God's claim to rulership. For this reason, in him the kingdom of God is present. Jesus' life, death, resurrection and exaltation stand as a demonstration of the claim of God to rulership. And he has been installed as Lord of the universe. This demonstration of God's rulership entails the demand that all persons acknowledge God as sovereign. Some obey that demand, confess Jesus as Lord and thereby enter the kingdom of God. Similarly, the principles of the kingdom are present in the world as a whole, seeking to permeate human society. As these principles are lived out, the kingdom of God is present.

Although the kingdom is here, this presence is partial and not yet consummated. For this reason there remains a future, eschatological aspect of the kingdom. One day all persons will acknowledge the lordship of Jesus (Phil 2:10-11). Likewise, one day the principles of God's kingdom will be universally actualized in the new human society that God will inaugurate. At that time God will be king over all the universe de facto. What is God's by right (de jure) will be actualized in the world. The entire universe will be the realm of God's rule.

In short, the kingdom of God comes as that order of peace, righteousness, justice and love that God gives to the world. This gift arrives in an ultimate way only at the eschaton, the renewal of the world brought by Jesus' return. But already the power of the kingdom is at work, for it breaks into the present from the future. Therefore, we can experience the kingdom in a partial yet real sense prior to the great eschatological day.

This then—the eschatological kingdom as the future of the world and its presence in the here-and-now—stands as an important theological motif, an illuminative and integrative theme for theological reflection. Around and with a view toward the reign of God, we can develop a helpful systematic delineation of the Christian faith. The concept of the divine reign offers a promising focal point for understanding the great Christian doctrines of God, humankind, Christ, the Spirit, the church and the last things.

Community as an Integrative Motif

Despite the appropriateness of the motif of the kingdom of God, this concept alone is insufficient to provide the unifying center for a revisioned evangelical theology. Kingdom theology suffers from at least one fatal flaw. It employs as its integrative motif a concept that it leaves undefined. The focus on the kingdom raises foundational questions that beg to be answered: What is the kingdom of God that is coming but is already present among us? What does it mean to speak of the reign of God? What is the experience of the rulership of God? What is the significance of Jesus' prayer "Your kingdom come, your will be done"? In short, what is the world like when it is transformed by the in-breaking of the kingdom?

When the content of the kingdom is left undefined, crucial questions such as these remain unaddressed.

Apart from the purely academic dimensions of these questions, leaving the concept of the kingdom undefined invites certain adverse practical implications. In the contemporary Western context, a contentless kingdom idea readily leads to a theology captivated by one of the destructive characteristics of the "spirit of our age," the emphasis on a radical, unbiblical individualism. Hence a theology of the kingdom easily degenerates into an individualistic theology—a theology that exalts and undergirds the extreme individualism of the modern era.

North American society is indeed imbued with individualism. The ethos of modern living orients itself toward the myth of the autonomous self. We elevate and celebrate the unencumbered individual, not always realizing that this concept comes more from modern philosophy, especially the legacy of Descartes, Locke and Hume, than from the Bible.

The elevation of the self is noticeable, for example, in our tendency to define ourselves fundamentally in terms of the choices we make. In this way we reveal our attempt to see ourselves as individual, autonomous, self-determining subjects. The autonomous self of the Western myth supposedly exists independently and entirely outside of any tradition or community, although the self may choose voluntarily to join some community.[29] According to Robert Bellah and his associates, writing in their seminal study *Habits of the Heart,* for most North Americans the meaning of life is "to become one's own person, almost to give birth to oneself."[30] Hence our society encourages us to "cut free from the past, to define our own selves, to choose the groups with which we wish to identify."[31] Bellah et al. depict the unencumbered self of Western individualism as the empty self, a concept perpetrated in the context of "the upward mobility of the middle-class individual who must leave home and church in order to succeed in an impersonal world of rationality and competition."[32]

According to Western thinking, the unencumbered, autonomous self not only is the essence of the individual person but also forms the foundation for the social orders, all of which are viewed from the vantage point of social atomism. The modern conception of the political order, for example, is based on the "social contract." According to this theory, autonomous selves come together to form the state. They contract with each other to give up certain personal prerogatives to the whole for the sake of personal advantage. The contract model finds its ecclesiological counterpart in the view of the church as a voluntary association of individual believers whose identity is not constituted by their presence in the congregation, but is fixed prior to their joining together.

Despite a gallant attempt to the contrary, nineteenth-century liberalism fell prey to the danger of individualistic theology. Liberalism was indeed a kingdom-oriented theology. By defining the kingdom in terms of the ethical society of persons of good will founded by Jesus, this theology focused its gaze on the social dimension of the kingdom. Nevertheless, liberalism floundered on the rocks of individualism, because it was unable to overcome the legacy of Schleiermacher, whose theology began with the God-consciousness of the individual. Consequently, liberal theology's society of persons of good will was in the final analysis merely an aggregate of individuals.

Leonard Sweet laments the ongoing outworkings of the liberal movement in Protestant churches. He writes,

> A tradition cannot long survive without a living memory. By failing to generate among church members a sense of living out of their past, much of Protestantism cut the cords of community in the present and endangered its survival. . . . But the labor of liberalism to give birth to

"community" failed in that era because of no tradition of meaning to build around. Just as one learns a language by living in community, so one learns the language of faith—what it means to live and think the Christian story—by living in Christian community. One of the main reasons for the widely lamented illiteracy about the language of faith in the churches, and the lack of consensus among the faithful about doctrinal matters, was this decline in Christian community due to the demise of the past.[33]

The situation produced by liberalism did not improve with the rejection of classical liberalism in the twentieth century. Rather than correcting the individualistic tendency evidenced in liberalism, the theological outworking of the rediscovery of apocalyptic only exacerbated the problem. In fact, the critique of the liberal understanding of the kingdom left the concept even more open to a purely individualistic interpretation. The kingdom of God, exegetes discovered, based as it is in the apocalyptic worldview, is the catastrophic action of God to bring the present order to a close and inaugurate the new order. But when read within the context of Western individualism, the eschatological new order could make no convincing claim for the necessity of a social dimension. As the eschatological rule of God, the kingdom could be simply a reality in which the individual as individual can participate. Twentieth-century theology, therefore, maintained—even deepened—the role of modern theology as the support for the cult of the individual.

There are signs, however, that the fascination with individualism that has characterized the modern Western era is waning. This development is unmistakably observable in the human sciences, which reveal a groundswell of interest in the concept of community. The strong appeal of this idea is due to several motivations.[34] But basically this interest is a result of a growing rejection of certain central features of modernity, especially its radical individualism. Many thinkers are now realizing that our understanding of the human phenomenon must reflect a more adequate balance between its individual and its social dimensions. Daniel A. Helminiak speaks for many in asserting that "the human phenomenon is always and simultaneously and inextricably both social and individual. . . . There is no human being apart from the social group in which he or she participates, and there is no group apart from the individual members who constitute that group."[35]

The current recognition of the importance of the social dimension of the human phenomenon has been developing over the last hundred years. It has led to the development of a new model of the relationship between the individual and society, called *communalism* or *culturalism*.[36] The precursors of the new communalism include some of the most prominent thinkers of the early twentieth century.[37]

Among the seminal voices calling for an emphasis on community were certain philosophers, including the turn-of-the-century thinkers Charles Peirce (1839-1914) and Josiah Royce (1855-1916).[38] In *The Problem of Christianity* Royce explored the idea of one vast "community of interpretation," not so much as a present reality but as a task to which we ought to be loyal. Anticipating contemporary writers such as Robert Bellah, he spoke of community in religious terms, as a community of memory and hope, faith and redeeming grace.[39]

But perhaps more influential than any philosopher have been the social scientists. Important to the rise of the new emphasis on community, for example, has been the work of French sociologist Emile Durkheim (1858-1917). Durkheim emphasized the group as the origin of the ideals of individuals, and he argued that rather than preceding collective life, the division of labor can arise only in the midst of a society. Social cohesion, he said, is facilitated by "collective representations," the group-based symbols with which individuals identify. Hence, a prerequisite to social diversification is a "conscious collective," a given solidarity of shared meanings and values.[40] The function of religion, in turn, is related to the symbols of a people. By providing such symbols, religion creates and maintains social solidarity.

Significant as well have been the ideas of George Herbert Mead (1863-1931). Foundational to Mead's contribution is his assertion that meaning is no individual matter but rather is interpersonal or relational. From theses such as these he inferred that the mind is not only individual but also a

social phenomenon.[41] In the same way, Mead argued that the self—the
maturing personality, or one's personal identity—is socially produced.[42]
These considerations led him to conclude that the individual is not *sui
generis*. Human development is a product of the process of social interaction, for the mind, critical thinking and a sense of self are facilitated by
participation in the social group.

These pioneering works lie at the foundation of the thinking of the late-
twentieth-century communalists, with their critique of modern individualism and their appeal to the concept of community. The fundamental short-
coming of the radical individualism of the West, they argue, is its disregard
for the social dimension of life and for the importance of that dimension
in the shaping of the self. Imbued as we are by the myth of the unencumbered self, they theorize, we do not see ourselves as discovering our per-
sonhood, our deepest beliefs and values—in short, our world—in and
through tradition and community. The prevailing individualism is simply
incorrect, critics argue. As Bellah et al. point out,

> There are truths we do not see when we adopt the language of radical
> individualism. We find ourselves not independently of other people and
> institutions but through them. We never get to the bottom of our selves
> on our own. We discover who we are face to face and side by side with
> others in work, love, and learning. All of our activity goes on in relation-
> ships, groups, associations, and communities ordered by institutional
> structures and interpreted by cultural patterns of meaning. . . . Finally,
> we are not simply ends in ourselves, either as individuals or as a society.
> We are parts of a larger whole that we can neither forget nor imagine
> in our own image without paying a high price.[43]

In contrast to radical individualism, the communalists emphasize the importance of the social unit—the community—for certain crucial aspects of
human living. For example, the community is integral to epistemology (the
process of knowing). Communalists argue that we can no longer hold to
the modern epistemological paradigm which focuses on the self-reflective,
autonomous subject. Rather, central to the knowing process is a cognitive
framework mediated to the individual by the community. In keeping with

this critique, contemporary social theorists are seeking to replace the individualistic foundational rationalism of modernism with an understanding of knowledge and belief that views them as socially and linguistically constituted.[44]

Similarly, communalists assert, the community is crucial to identity formation. Critics of individualism argue that a sense of personal identity develops through the telling of a personal narrative. Hence finding ourselves means, among other things, finding the story or narrative in terms of which our lives make sense.[45] The fundamental correctness of this thesis is borne out by the popular interest in schemes of "life stages" or life crises as a means of providing coherence for the otherwise arbitrary experiences people undergo. Communalists declare that the story of a person's life is always embedded in the story of the communities in which the person participates,[46] for traditions mediated by communities, not individuals, are the carriers of rationality. The transcending story is mediated to the individual by the community, which transmits from generation to generation and from group to individual traditions of virtue, common good and ultimate meaning.[47] Consequently, if the concept of the "course of life" is to provide meaning, we must set it within a larger generational, historical and religious—that is, community—context.[48]

Although epistemology and identity formation may form primary examples, contemporary communalists argue that the community is also crucial to the sustaining of character, virtue and values. And it provides the necessary foundation for involvement in public discourse concerning matters of worldview. Consequently, not only is community integral to the formation of the individual identity, but it is also crucial to the well-being of the broader society. Communalists argue that a society is not merely an aggregate of individuals. Instead, foundational to society are the communities that transmit traditions from one generation to another. Bellah and associates speak for the new thinking:

> In short, we have never been, and still are not, a collection of private individuals who, except for a conscious contract to create a minimal government, have nothing in common. Our lives make sense in a thou-

sand ways, most of which we are unaware of, because of traditions that are centuries, if not millennia, old. It is these traditions that help us to know that it does make a difference who we are and how we treat one another.[49]

Bellah et al. offer one crucial warning, however. We must not confuse "community" with what they perceptively term a "lifestyle enclave."[50] Lifestyle enclaves, they note, are segmental, involving only a segment of each individual—the private life, especially leisure and consumption—and including only those that share a particular lifestyle. In other words, a lifestyle enclave is a group of persons who are united merely by shared interests and activities. A community, in contrast, "attempts to be an inclusive whole, celebrating the interdependence of public and private life and of the different callings of all."

Nor is community to be confused with the older strand of American thought that sees social life as merely an arrangement for the fulfillment of individuals' needs. This view is found in the contemporary "therapeutic" conception of "communities of interest," groups of self-interested individuals who join together to maximize individual good.[51]

In steering us away from these mistaken notions, Bellah and associates offer a helpful starting point. A community, they write, "is a group of people who are socially interdependent, who participate together in discussion and decision making, and who share certain *practices* . . . that both define the community and are nurtured by it."[52] Such a community is oriented toward the past, the future and the present, and through this threefold orientation it constitutes the "self" of its members.

The past orientation of a community allows us, reminiscent of the thought of Josiah Royce, to speak of a "community of memory." A community has a history—in fact, it is in an important sense constituted by its past. Consequently a community does not forget its past. To keep the past alive a community retells its story—its constitutive narrative—and thereby it offers examples of persons who have embodied and exemplified the meaning of the community. In addition a community tells stories of shared suffering and even of past evils.[53]

But a community does not only turn its members toward the past; its gaze is also toward the future, so that it becomes a community of hope. It anticipates its own continuation and further development in the future. The community senses that it is moving forward toward an ideal that is yet to be.

By looking at the past and the future, a community provides a transcendent vantage point for life in the present. It supplies a context of meaning that can allow its members to connect their personal aspirations with those of a larger whole. It facilitates them in seeing their efforts as contributions to that whole.

A community is concerned to give a qualitative meaning to life, time and space, persons and groups. It is especially fitted for this task insofar as it does not view time merely as a continuous flow of qualitatively meaningless sensations. By punctuating the day, the week, the season, the year with a sense of the sacred, a community presents time as a meaningful whole.[54] A community also perpetuates "practices of commitment." These define the community way of life and the patterns of loyalty and obligation that keep the community alive.[55]

The human sciences are moving beyond the radical individualism of the modern era to an understanding that seeks to strike a balance between the individual and social dimensions of the human phenomenon. This development suggests that a revisioned evangelical theology may make a corresponding move. We must journey beyond the sole focus on the kingdom that typified the past orientation of theology, without leaving the insights of kingdom theology behind. The revisioned evangelicalism would incorporate into the reigning kingdom theology the motif of "community" as defining the nature of God's reign. This would permit the concept of the kingdom of God to be filled with its proper content.

The rationale for the emphasis on community found in the social sciences is strong. Thus the cultural pillar of theology is leading us to consider this concept as a crucial theme for use in systematic theology. More significant, however, is the *biblical* rationale for the incorporation of the concept of community.

"Community" is important as an integrative motif for theology not only because it fits with contemporary thinking concerning the nature of the world and the human phenomenon but, more important, because it is central to the message of the Bible. From the narratives of the primordial garden, which open the curtain on the biblical story, to the vision of white-robed multitudes inhabiting the new earth with which the story concludes, the drama of the Scriptures speaks of community.

But can we say more about the actual nature of the community God is seeking to construct? Taken as a whole, the Bible asserts that God's program is directed to bringing about community in the highest sense of the word—a redeemed people, living within a redeemed creation and enjoying the presence of their Redeemer God.

The vision of community as spelled out in the biblical drama begins in the past. God's intent is articulated already in the Genesis 2 narrative, as God notes, "It is not good for the man to be alone." The divine activity throughout history is directed toward bringing into being the community envisioned by the Creator who noted the solitariness of the first human in the Garden of Eden.

Central to the divine purpose of establishing community is the presence of God among his people. God's presence is a constant theme of the Bible. The Lord communed with Adam and Eve in the Garden. At various times and in various locations the patriarchs experienced the presence of God, and to commemorate their encounters with him they built landmarks, altars and memorials (e.g., Gen 28:13-17).

With a view toward the establishment of community—God dwelling with his people—God elected and entered into covenant with Israel. God's intent is evident in the exodus experience. The immediate goal of God's deliverance of Israel from the bondage of Egypt was the assembly of the people at Sinai. There God brought the Israelites into his presence, in order that they might be constituted as his people (Ex 20:2-3), among whom God himself would come to dwell. During the wilderness sojourn, God intended to make his abode among them in the tabernacle; his house, like theirs, would be a tent. So important was the presence of God among Israel that when God proposed that the tabernacle not be built because of Israel's sin, Moses responded, "If your Presence does not go with us, do not send us up from here" (Ex 33:15).[56] Later, when Israel established fixed dwellings in the Promised Land, God also put his glory within a house, the temple in Jerusalem.

The Old Testament experience forms the context for the significance of Jesus Christ as Immanuel—God with us (Mt 1:22-23). In Jesus, the divine Word became flesh and "tabernacled" among us (Jn 1:14); in him, God is present with humankind. Jesus promised that both he and the Father would take up their dwelling with his disciples; he spoke of another Comforter who would be present among his disciples (Jn 14:23, 26).

Jesus' promise, understood within the context of the Old Testament hope, forms the foundation for the work of the Spirit. Since his outpouring at Pentecost, the Holy Spirit facilitates the fulfillment of Jesus' assurance of his continual presence with his followers. The Holy Spirit constitutes them individually and corporately as the temple of God. Because of the finished work of Christ and the continuing work of the Holy Spirit, therefore, God himself is indeed among his people, even though our experience of that presence may be partial.

But the grand fulfillment of God's program lies yet in the future. The biblical story does not end with Pentecost, nor with the true, yet partial experience of the presence of God currently enjoyed by Christ's disciples. The drama of the Bible reaches from the past into the future. It reaches its climax with the grand vision of the new heaven and new earth.

The future renewed creation was anticipated by certain Old Testament prophets. But it is developed more fully by the closing chapters of the book of Revelation. The inspired seer looked to an era beyond the present, which will mark the completion of the divine program in human history. The seer pictured the new order as the new Jerusalem (Rev 21:9-21). In that city, the peoples of the new earth will live together in peace. Nature will again fulfill its purpose of providing nourishment for all earthly inhabitants (Rev 22:1-4). Most glorious of all, however, God will dwell with humans, thereby bringing to completion the ultimate divine design for creation:

And I heard a loud voice from the throne saying, "Now the dwelling of God is with men, and he will live with them. They will be his people, and God himself will be with them and be their God. . . ." The throne of God and of the Lamb will be in the city, and his servants will serve him. They will see his face, and his name will be on their foreheads. (Rev 21:3; 22:3-4)

Hence the future new order will be characterized by community in the fullest sense. The participants in the eschatological reality will live in fellowship with each other, with creation and, most important, with God.

The centrality of John's vision of a future eon characterized by a new community of reconciliation, fellowship and harmony confirms the assertion that the establishment of community lies at the heart of the concern of the Bible. God's ultimate intention is not a transpositioning of the individual believer to an isolated, individual realm of unending "eternal life" beyond the world and time. Rather, God's program focuses on the corporate human story, and therefore on humans as potential participants in a new society in the coming eon. In fact, Scripture consistently presents our eternal home in social rather than individual terms. It is a great city, it encompasses many dwelling places, it is composed of a multitude of inhabitants. Hence it is a social reality. As Paul Hanson notes from his study of the theme of community in the Bible, "God's future reign was not construed in terms of a blissful union of the elect with God that removed them from the world of humanity, but as a reign of justice and peace that repaired all wounds and restored righteousness as the standard among humans."[57]

The vision of the Scriptures is clear: the final goal of the work of the triune God in salvation history is the establishment of the eschatological community—a redeemed people dwelling in a renewed earth, enjoying reconciliation with their God, fellowship with each other and harmony with all creation. Consequently, the goal of community lies at the heart of God's actions in history.

The social nature of God's intent is displayed likewise in the focal point of salvation history, the Christ event. Jesus came as the exemplary human being, the revelation of who we are to be. And the divine design revealed by Jesus focuses on our living in relationship with God and with others. Jesus also came as the Messiah—a social figure, the fulfillment of the hopes and aspirations of the Hebrew people and, by extension, of all humankind. In the same way, his intent was not to fulfill an individual vocation for his own sake, but to be obedient to the will of the Father for the sake of humankind. Thus in his death he took upon himself the sins of all, and he rose from the grave in order to mediate to us eternal life through our union with him.

The work of the Holy Spirit likewise has the establishment of community in view. His outpouring at Pentecost was directed toward the establishing of the corporate body of Christ to be the one new people composed of Jews and Gentiles reconciled to each other (Eph 2:11-22). During the present age the Holy Spirit is bringing together a people that transcends every human division—a people from every nation and every socioeconomic status, and consisting of both male and female (Gal 3:28).

The completed work of Christ and the present work of the Spirit mean that the eschatological community that arrives in its fullness only at the consummation of human history is already present among us in a partial, yet genuine, manner. This present reality is to be experienced in many ways, but its focal point is the community of the followers of Christ. The Christian church is a distinctive body formed by God through the life, death and resurrection of Jesus,[58] a community of faith that transcends spatial and temporal boundaries.

The New Testament writers, such as Paul, declare that to be a Christian means fundamentally to be united with Christ. This union with Christ entails not only mentally assenting to a set of doctrines but also embodying in our beliefs, attitudes and actions the meanings and values that characterized Jesus' own life. In this process of embodiment the Christian faith community is crucial. The believing community transmits from generation to generation and region to region the redemptive story, which it recounts in word and deed. In so doing it mediates to us as believers the framework for the formation of our personal identity, values and worldview.

Through their loyalty to Christ and within the context of the faith community, Christians enjoy a common life marked by unity with Jesus. In this common life we seek to be a true community of faith, which community we manifest in corporate worship, mutual edification and outreach to the world. The worship dimension focuses the attention of the believing community on the One who constitutes us as his people. Through the corporate worship life, the community also gathers to commemorate the foundational events of our spiritual existence, at the center of which is the action of God in Christ delivering humankind from the bondage of sin.

The dimension of edification means that as the corporate people we take seriously our existence as a fellowship of mutuality. Community therefore means that we sense our oneness with each other. We enter into a relationship of sympathy, compassion, empathy. We intercede for each other, care for each other and minister to each other's needs. The demands of the life of discipleship in a fundamentally inhospitable context heighten the importance of mutuality. We desperately need the support of others who share the same vision of God's actions in the world and who are also dedicated to participation in the divine activity.

No true community of faith, however, can fail to direct its sights outward, toward the world in which it is called to live. Foundational to its existence is a vision of the whole human family reconciled to God, one another and creation. Consequently, we direct our energies toward those who are beyond our community membership; we seek to proclaim the gospel and minister to the hurts of needy people. And we hold up before the world the sovereignty of God as the only hope, and the only sure alternative to the myriad competing loyalties which despite their lure fall short of ultimacy.

At the center of the transmission of the redemptive story worked out in the life of the believing community is the Bible, the book of the church. The Bible remains central to the faith and life of the contemporary believing community exactly *because* we see ourselves as an extension of the biblical community of faith. This book is in effect our spiritual autobiography,[59] tracing the birth, pilgrimage and vision of the ancient faith community in which we participate. Consequently, we study the Scriptures in order to discern what it means to be the community of faith, and hence what it means to be the community of faith today.

Related to the biblical proclamation are the rites of the community, specifically baptism and the Lord's Supper. These two sacraments reenact the story of redemption—both as they memorialize the events of Jesus' passion and resurrection and as they bear testimony to the experience of union with Christ shared by the entire community.

Baptism marks our initiation into the narrative of the Christian community. This practice inducts the new believer into the shared practices of the community that is defined and ruled by the story of Christ's life, death and resurrection.[60] The church, therefore, rightly sees in baptism the symbol of the new birth and the new identity that initiates into the church enjoy. For baptism represents the change of context that has resulted in the believer's now belonging to the family of God. No longer do we define our lives in accordance with the categories of the old life. Rather, we see ourselves as those who have passed from the rulership of sin and its condemnation into the people of God, who enjoy reconciliation with our Lord and Savior and therefore with each other. The new identity symbolized by our baptism carries ethical demands. We must now live out in our conduct the new identity God has freely bestowed on us: we must be the community of God which we are.

What is initially declared in baptism is repeatedly articulated by the other rite of the church, the Lord's Supper. By our participation in this sacrament, we are reminded of our identity in Christ, our covenant with God and one another, and the resultant ethical demand that we live "unto the Lord."

Conclusion: Kingdom and Community

In seeking a revisioned evangelical theology, we do well to orient our discussion of the Christian faith around the twin motifs of the reign of God and the community of God. The Bible presents history as meaningful, in that it is directed toward a goal—the kingdom of God or the presence of the will of God throughout the earth. This goal forms the central petition of the Lord's Prayer: "Your kingdom come, your will be done on earth as it is in heaven" (Mt 6:10). The incorporation of the idea of community as an integrative motif for theology does not mark a rejection of this concept of the kingdom of God. It is not a *retreat* from the discussions of the twentieth century; rather, the inclusion of "community" as an integrative motif for theology marks a move *beyond* the older paradigm. The concept of community fills the concept of the kingdom of God with its proper content. When God's rule is present—that is, when God's will is done—community emerges. Or viewed from the opposite direction, in the emergence of community God's rule is present and God's will is accomplished.

As it exists in the world the community of faith is, in fact, a laboratory of the kingdom. We seek to embody the vision of God's new order, to reflect those qualities that we infer from God's activities on behalf of creation. As a people who have experienced God's gracious deliverance from bondage and God's marvelous reconciliation, we are free to show forth the nature of the liberating God and thereby give witness to the state of affairs that characterizes the in-breaking of God's reign.

The kingdom of God, therefore, is the vision of God's ruling presence that redeems, reconciles and transforms creation into God's intended ideal and constitutes the world as God's realm. It both transcends history and works within history as the paradigm of the new order and the power effecting that order. It is, in the words of Peter Hodgson, "the way God *acts* redemptively, efficaciously in the world."[61] This biblical vision, however, is communal or social in scope. The kingdom of God is characterized by community. It is present wherever the new society of reconciliation is created—that people who have entered into covenant with the God of history and consequently live out their covenantal life through worship of the God revealed in Christ, through mutual care and through mission in and for the world.

7
REVISIONING THE CHURCH

Let us return to the example with which I launched the introduction to this book. In a February 1991 memo, the executive minister of a North American Baptist denomination listed the concerns that would be taken up at the fall meeting of the denominational think tank on faith, order and identity. The list was fascinating for what it excluded. None of the perplexing questions concerning the triunity of God, the two natures of Christ, the transmission of sin, the doctrine of Scripture or the events surrounding Christ's Second Coming were on the list. Instead, the questions to be addressed had to do with church membership, baptism, ordination and organizational structure; all focused on the doctrine of the church.

Congregations of many denominational traditions find themselves dealing with issues similar to those pinpointed by the Baptist leader—matters previous generations assumed had been settled. Once again at issue, for example, is the nature of church membership. Evangelicals today are unsure not only about the link between baptism and joining the church, but whether congregations should continue formal membership at all. The questioning of the traditional understanding of church membership is evident in the current phenomenon of "church-hopping." Many people no longer see themselves as permanent members of a particular congregation, but flit from one church to another almost capriciously.

At issue in many congregations as well is church government. Old structures are breaking down. The diminishing attendance at church business meetings indicates that an increasing number of people are uninvolved in formal decision making. But many absentees nevertheless become decision makers after the fact, "voting" with their financial contributions and attendance whether or not to support what "the church" has decided to do.

Worship style has likewise emerged as a crucial issue. It is coupled with another—the immense expectations people have for their church. Many have come to believe that the local congregation exists to provide services to its clientele, and the church is sharply criticized when it fails to perform according to expectations. For example, some people, influenced by contemporary "renewal" voices, expect the church to be a place for healing. And they express frustration when they fail to find in their local congregation the anticipated "demonstrations of power."

In the midst of the ferment, leaders representing many denominations are calling for a renewed emphasis on the biblical doctrine of the church. Andrew Kuyvenhoven of the Canadian Christian Reformed Church speaks for many concerned pastors when he writes concerning the current indifference toward denominational identity:

> The most painful negative feature of this new tolerance of denominations is the underlying theological indifference toward the biblical teaching about the church. We simply have a poorly defined ecclesiology. Evangelicals tend to believe that a personal relationship to Jesus is the one thing that counts. At their meetings they have been told that mem-

bership in a church cannot save a person, that baptism cannot save, that the Lord's supper is not magic, and that personal conscience is greater than the rules of any church assembly. For them the church exists for personal growth and as a means for mission.[1]

Similarly, concerned theologians suggest that the current churning of the ecclesiological waters is the outworking of the lack of serious work in ecclesiology among evangelicals. For some time the doctrine of the church has been the neglected stepchild of evangelical theology. Cognizant of this, several theologians[2] have chastised the movement for its omission of an ecclesiology from its doctrinal base.

This omission is perhaps understandable, given the nature of the evangelical coalition that emerged in the second half of the twentieth century. D. A. Carson summarizes the situation:

> The doctrinal and ethical concerns that tie together the diverse branches of evangelicalism have little to do with ecclesiology *per se*. There are many evangelicals who have written usefully and provocatively on the church, but by and large it is not their evangelicalism that has prompted them to do so. In short, evangelicalism as a movement is much more defined by Christology, soteriology and bibliology than by ecclesiology.[3]

At the same time, as Carson indicates, because the doctrine of the church overarches many areas of disagreement among evangelicals, they may have in fact "produced too many ecclesiologies."[4] The problem, therefore, is not that evangelicals have no shared ecclesiology; rather the very nature of the evangelical coalition has demanded that they settle for a truncated doctrine of the church. Hence Clark Pinnock correctly notes a neglect of "the ecclesial nature of Christianity."[5] And Nathan Hatch rightly calls for a recovery of "a higher view of the church."[6]

The contemporary evangelical ferment concerning the church confirms the opinion of one British evangelical. Although there is a certain weakness and lack of clarity in the way evangelicals theologize about the church, Melvin Tinker notes, they "have been giving a great deal of time to thinking about the church . . . from a more practical point of view."[7] Consequently, the current situation offers us an opportunity to rethink our ecclesiology in a more concerted, systematic fashion.

The conclusions of chapter six point in the same direction: the emphasis on the kingdom of God must be augmented through an exploration of community. Of the implications entailed in such an augmentation, none is more vital or far-reaching than the revitalizing of ecclesiology. A revisioning of evangelical theology, therefore, demands that evangelical thinkers give proper place to defining the nature and task of the church, in order to meet the challenge of the new century.

But what form would such a redefining take? To come to grips with this matter, we must first get clear in our sights the crisis we face in the contemporary church.

The Crisis in the Contemporary Church

Contemporary evangelical life reflects a movement in the midst of an identity crisis. Recent social and ecclesiological trends have caught us off-balance, calling into question our traditional identity without helping us generate a renewed sense of who we are.

A malaise, a crisis of identity, has engulfed the evangelical movement. But the situation is not uniquely ours. Mainline Protestantism has known uncertainty for several years, as is evidenced in its unabated decline in church membership. Even more communitarian groups have felt the shattering of the older stability. Recent Mennonite writings, for example, reflect a people struggling with the loss of their traditional ecclesiology.[8] Similarly, Roman Catholic hierarchies are breaking down under the onslaught of "progressive" thinking[9] and widespread dismissal of official pronouncements by both leaders and laity.

In recent years, evangelicals have grown dissatisfied with old patterns of church life and the old consensus concerning the nature of the church. In increasing numbers Christians are forsaking the evangelical middle ground and moving ecclesiologically to the left or the right.

Exercising a powerful leftward thrust are the waves of the charismatic movement that repeatedly churn religious waters. This movement, with its radically low view of the church, reflects an undefined, fluid ecclesiology.

For those who catch the new spirit, ecclesiastical structures, church affiliations, sacramental acts and fellowship with like-minded Christians are less important than the affinity they sense with like-experienced, "Spirit-filled" believers. Charismatics have grown tired of the "blandness" of traditional evangelicalism.

The rightward pull arises from the opposite direction, from the traditional or liturgical churches. In recent years several prominent and many rank-and-file evangelicals have set out on the Canterbury Trail, walked the Roman Road or traversed the Highway to Constantinople. Rediscovering a high view of the church mediated through tradition and liturgy, these seekers hope to regain the continuity with the past they sense is lacking in the ad hoc ecclesiology of evangelicalism.

These two basic ecclesiologies, drawing evangelicals into what for them are new forms, move in diametrically opposite directions. Yet high church liturgicalism and charismatic informalism share certain elements. One of these common characteristics is unhealthy and bothersome. The pull to both the left and the right is readily connected with the radical individualism of contemporary Western culture which has been one factor in the steady undermining of the older concept of steadfast, self-sacrificial commitment.

In our society, commitments—from contracts to personal relationships—have lost the long-term perspective characteristic of the past. People today enter into short-term agreements for the sake of personal expedience. Based on personal profit—"what I can get"—these arrangements are fragile, easily broken by adverse circumstances or readily dismissed when they have outlived their perceived usefulness.

The cultural shift away from permanence toward expedience has been carried over into church life. In *Habits of the Heart,* Robert Bellah and his associates document the presence of individualism in people's attitudes about religion:

Most Americans see religion as something individual, prior to any organizational involvement. . . .

Yet important as the local church is to many Americans, it is not

identical with what is understood by *religion*, which has a meaning that transcended the individual and the local congregation. It is one of those differentiated spheres into which modern life is divided and which is largely handed over to "experts" who profess to understand it.[10]
Donald Bloesch sounds a similar note, claiming that the "appalling neglect" of ecclesiology in evangelicalism is due in part to the emphasis on individual decision, as evangelicals give priority to the decision of faith rather than to nurture.[11]

The loss of commitment under the rubric of individualism is readily evident in the disturbing demise of the sense of loyalty to congregation and denomination that increasingly marks the evangelical movement. This loosening of loyalty is one factor that has opened the door for the exodus of evangelicals into older traditions and newer experiments, both of which promise to supply what they perceive to be lacking in their former churches.

A more profound relationship between this hallmark of contemporary culture and the tug away from the middle, however, begs to be noted. On the surface, the recent surge of evangelicals into the churches oriented toward tradition appears to be a reaction against the trends of society around us. By embracing high church Anglicanism, Roman Catholicism or Eastern Orthodoxy, evangelical Christians gain the sense that they are now linked with an ecclesiastical reality that spans the centuries, and thereby they are lodging a protest against the rootlessness associated with individualism and the breakdown of commitment. But on another level, the migration to the right, just as much as the shift to the left, can actually be a move toward individualism and away from commitment. The view that believers are initiated into a corporate life in which they are to become personally involved and over which they are to take personal ownership invests membership with great responsibility. If the people are the church, ongoing congregational life demands the involvement of each member in a way that the leader-centered polity of both the liturgical churches and the newer charismatic groups often does not allow.

Regardless of whether the new traditionalism and the new fluidity are reactions to or indicative of contemporary culture, they do signal a dissatisfaction with evangelical ecclesiology. Both can exhibit a deep-seated desire for a new understanding of the relationship between the personal life of faith and the faith community, and for recapturing a sense of participation in the worship life of the community, which the evangelical middle has tended to deemphasize. In fact, perhaps the greatest longings of today's restless Christians are to know how they fit within the larger whole and to engage in meaningful worship of their Creator and Savior.

The current longings for a sense of participation in something larger than the mundane and for a sense of the presence of God in the worship life of the church may form the most significant word the Spirit is speaking today to evangelicalism. Contemporary currents and countercurrents indicate that the older ecclesiological forms are losing their ability to provide Christians with direction in their search for God and their quest to be God's family in the world.

The strong sense of corporateness and the heightened awareness of the presence of God that people find lacking cannot be recovered apart from a renewal of the broader understanding of the nature of the church—a renewal in ecclesiology. We cannot simply return to the ecclesiology of the past. But neither ought we to be theological chameleons, changing our skin color with our environment. Our task is to look to the Scriptures and bring together the best from our heritage and the ferment of our time. We must employ these resources in the attempt to construct a doctrine of the church that is biblical, evangelical and contemporary.

Foundational Motifs in Ecclesiology

On what basis can we engage in the task of reconstructing ecclesiology? What forms the foundation for a renewed vision of who we are as the church of Jesus Christ?

Although some prefer to begin with the church's mission,[12] most evangelical theologians develop responses to the more practical questions concerning church life on a theoretical foundation focusing on the nature of the church. The latter is, of course, a proper way of proceeding. But among thinkers who follow this method, there is no unanimity as to how to set

forth the basic meaning of the church. Nevertheless, four distinct motifs—
whether used singly or in combination with each other—are widely employed in evangelical writings.[13]

Some theologians, elevating the New Testament understanding as the
norm, look to the etymology of the Greek word translated "church"—*ekklēsia*—to provide the foundational motif for ecclesiology.[14] Because the
term arises from the verb *kaleō* (to call) to which has been added the
preposition *ek* (out of), they conclude, *ekklēsia* means "the called-out ones."

Although in general etymology forms a tenuous court of appeal, the
employment of the term as a foundation for a doctrine of the church does
have some merit. For example, because *ekklēsia* is used in the Septuagint to
translate the Hebrew word *qāhāl* (assembly), the word provides a link to the
Old Testament. *Qāhāl,* in turn, carries special significance when used in
conjunction with Yahweh. As the people of God, Israel constituted the
"congregation" or the "assembly of the Lord" (Deut 23:1-8; 1 Chron 28:8).
This Old Testament concept might have formed the background for Jesus'
declaration that he would build his church, his congregation (Mt 16:18;
18:17). *Ekklēsia* also provides a link to the secular Roman world. This connection is visible in the New Testament itself, where the term occasionally
retains its general meaning. Hence *ekklēsia* refers to an assembly of people,
a group of persons called together for a specific purpose (Acts 19:32, 39,
41). In Roman society the citizens of a given community could be called
together to tend to city affairs, forming thereby an *ekklēsia.*

The term *ekklēsia,* therefore, indicates the self-consciousness of the early
Christians. They saw themselves as the continuation of what God had begun in the wilderness with the nation of Israel. They were that company
called together by the proclamation of the gospel for the purpose of belonging to God through Christ by the power of the Holy Spirit. In fact, so
strong is the biblical rootage of this concept that it forms a point of unity
for the community of faith across the Testaments. As Paul Hanson concludes from his study of the biblical concept of community,

> the community of faith in the Bible is the people *called.* It is the people
> *called* forth from diverse sorts of bondage to freedom, *called* to a sense

of identity founded on a common bond with the God of righteousness and compassion, and *called* to the twin vocations of worship and participation in the creative, redemptive purpose that unifies all history and is directed to the restoration of the whole creation within a universal order of *shalom*.[15]

The choice of *ekklēsia* as the designation of the Christian community carries an important implication for ecclesiology. It suggests that the New Testament Christians viewed the church as neither hierarchy nor edifice, but people—a people brought together by the Spirit to belong to God through Christ. Not only has this understanding been a vital part of evangelical thinking, but it has also generated broad consensus among the mainline churches in recent years.[16] The ecumenical document *Baptism, Eucharist and Ministry* affirms: "The Holy Spirit unites in a single body those who follow Jesus Christ and sends them as witnesses into the world. Belonging to the Church means living in communion with God through Jesus Christ in the Holy Spirit."[17]

A second biblical foundation upon which theologians build their doctrine of the church is made up of various New Testament metaphors concerning the church. Most often used are three such metaphors, each of which is related to one of the three members of the Trinity.[18]

The New Testament speaks of the church as God's people (2 Cor 6:16) and as God's nation and holy priesthood (1 Pet 2:9). This metaphor can be readily connected with the Old Testament rootage of *ekklēsia*. Just as Israel had been chosen to be the people of God, so now the New Testament church enjoys this relationship. But there is one important difference. No longer is status as God's nation based on membership within a specific ethnic group—the physical descendants of Abraham. Now people from the entire world are called together to belong to God, for the church is an international fellowship comprising persons "from every tribe and language and people and nation" (Rev 5:9).

Whereas "people" and "nation" focus on status, "priesthood" connotes function. This term too is rooted in, while forming a contrast to, the Old Testament. In ancient Israel certain persons carried out prescribed priestly functions, and these continue in the New Testament era, albeit on a different level. But whereas in Israel only a few were selected from among the people to act as priests, in the church all the people of God belong to the priestly order, and the ministry of the priesthood is shared by all.[19] The authors of *Baptism, Eucharist and Ministry* express the contemporary convergence on this matter: "Jesus Christ is the unique priest of the new covenant. . . . Derivatively the Church as a whole can be described as a priesthood. All members are called to offer their being 'as a living sacrifice' and to intercede for the Church and the salvation of the world."[20]

The New Testament also speaks of the church as the body of Christ (Eph 1:22-23; 1 Cor 12:27), of which he is the head (Col 1:18). The background of this picture is not found so much in the Old Testament as in human anatomy. Both the relationship of the physical body to its head and the organic unity present in the human body signify what is to be true of the church.[21] As Christ's body, the church exists solely to do his will. It is to follow the dictates of the Lord and thereby be the vehicle of carrying out his will. In this way, the church is the presence of Christ in the world. And like the human body, the church is a unity made up of diversity (see 1 Cor 12:1-31). Not all have the same function, but all have the same goal; all members are to be concerned for all others and use their gifts in service to the whole.

According to the New Testament, the church is likewise the temple of the Holy Spirit (Eph 2:19-22; 1 Pet 2:9). This metaphor also arises out of the Old Testament. In Israel a temple was erected to be in some special way God's earthly dwelling place (1 Chron 6:1-2). Now, however, the focal point of God's presence is the fellowship of his people. The presence of the Holy Spirit carries grave ethical consequence. It means that Christians are to live holy lives (1 Cor 6:19-20).

Rather than direct appeal to New Testament teaching for the foundation of ecclesiology, certain thinkers opt for a more systematic-theological approach. Some begin with the perceived manifestations of the church—that is, the classical differentiation between the universal or invisible church and the local, individual or visible church.[22] Despite its long pedigree in the church as a whole and within evangelicalism, this distinction is coming under increasing fire today. As D. A. Carson notes, it is "either fundamentally mistaken, or at best of marginal importance."[23]

Perhaps more helpful than the classical twofold distinction is a three-part delineation—the mystical church, the universal church and the local churches. The "mystical church" encompasses all believers of all ages (Heb 12:22-23) and as such has a unity that transcends time. The "universal church" consists of all believers on earth at any given time, a concept that highlights a unity that transcends space. And the "local church," of course, is the visible company of believers gathered in a specific place.

Within evangelicalism, the Baptists have been most noted for holding high the banner of the local church, based on their claim that the New Testament places greatest emphasis precisely here. But in recent years the local church has gained a heightened stature among evangelicals from other denominations as well. In an article in *Perspectives,* Reformed Church pastor Allan Janssen makes the bold assertion that *"all* church is local."[24] Building from the Reformation understanding of the event character of the church, he chastises his colleagues for what he sees as the docetic "flight from the local." And he calls on his readers to take more seriously both the people who meet together in the local congregation and the local setting in which they are called to serve.

The emphasis on the local church is surely correct. But while highlighting the importance of the visible fellowship of believers, we dare not forget that each local congregation derives its significance from its participation in and representation of the common whole.[25] It is to be nothing less than the visible expression of the one church of Jesus Christ and therefore the church of Jesus Christ in miniature.

Despite the growing ecclesiological emphasis on the local church, the dominant thinking within evangelicalism moves in the opposite direction. Implicit in evangelical ecclesiology is a focus on the universal church as the invisible company of the elect, and consequently, albeit not necessarily intentionally, many evangelicals have little place for the local church. Already in 1968 Klaas Runia, citing W. Stanford Reid, noted this tendency. Among the causes of the current intellectual floundering among evangelicals, he points to an erroneous doctrine of the church, for many evangelicals "tend to regard the visible organised Church as relatively unimportant."[26]

The typical evangelical deemphasis of the local church has several causes. One is the influence of the older dispensationalism within the movement. Dallas Seminary theologian Robert Lightner stands as an example of this thinking when he declares that the "company of the redeemed is called the church without consideration of whether or not those who are a part of it are members of local churches."[27] For Lightner, membership in the universal, invisible church comes through union with Christ, which is accomplished solely through Spirit baptism. Water baptism, in turn, is but "an ordinance of the local church." It is merely "the means by which one's union with Christ in his death, burial, and resurrection is made public."[28]

Writing in the *Grace Theological Journal,* Michael D. Williams bemoans the tendency among dispensationalists to elevate the invisible church at the expense of the local congregation. He alleges that the dispensationalist emphasis on the individual believer and the mystical, transcendent nature of the church has "minimized to the point of unimportance" the believer's inclusion in the visible church. Consequently, "the church as the concrete assembling of the body of Christ, the body of believers that you or I assemble with as the church . . . has tended to be of negligible importance in dispensational theology."[29]

But another theological factor may shoulder even greater responsibility for the elevation of the invisible church in evangelicalism. The Mennonite theologian C. Norman Kraus claims that evangelical ecclesiology is based on the presuppositions and definitions of a Calvinist view of divine election and the invisibility of true faith. Consequently, Kraus links evangelicalism's truncated understanding of the church to an inadequate soteriology. Evangelicals individualize and privatize salvation, defining it in terms of a theological affirmation of belief in Christ, exclusive of social dimensions. As a result of its abridged soteriology, he concludes, evangelicalism lacks an ecclesiology that can undergird a church of disciples.[30]

Kraus's criticism finds echo among evangelical critics of the older ecclesiology. Clark Pinnock, for example, likewise links evangelicalism's deficient ecclesiology to a truncated soteriology. He writes concerning the movement in which he claims membership, "We give the impression that all that interests us is the justification of individual sinners and not their sanctification or the institution of the church or the sanctification of the world."[31]

Another cause of evangelicalism's insufficient ecclesiology is less intellectual or theological than practical. The postfundamentalist evangelical coalition that came into existence in the mid-twentieth century is by necessity transdenominational. In order to enlist support for the crucial tasks to which they sensed themselves called—including defending orthodoxy in the face of the challenge of liberalism and neo-orthodoxy, and launching a bold new thrust in evangelism—our evangelical forebears needed to bring into the coalition persons of varying denominational loyalties. To this end, they followed the nineteenth-century model of voluntary societies and established a panorama of parachurch organizations. These facilitated their desire to circumvent the sticky issues of denominational polity that could so easily derail the evangelical program. But the move toward transdenominational voluntary societies also served to loosen the cords of denominational loyalty and even to lead some of the new organizations—against the initial intent of their founders—to function in quasi-church or quasi-denominational manners.

The new evangelicalism with its goal of fostering a broad coalition of believers and its fledgling parachurch organizations required a new doctrine of the church. The emerging ecclesiology focused on a spiritual unity enjoyed by individual believers which transcends the visible churches. Christ can have loyal followers in any and all denominations, evangelicals claim, and these loyal followers constitute the true church, the only *ecclesia* that is of ultimate importance.

There are promising signs that the inordinate emphasis on the invisible church with its deprecation of the visible expression is beginning to wane in evangelical circles. Increasingly evangelical thinkers are echoing Bloesch's call for "a passionate concern for church unity," understood as "not only spiritual but visible unity."[32] This concern can only lead beyond the former ecclesiology toward the goal of restoring the church to its rightful place in the world.

The distinction between the invisible and visible church, with the corresponding elevation of the invisible church, has served as a distinctively evangelical response to the question of ecclesiology. More widespread in theology as a whole as a systematic-theological foundation for the doctrine of the church, however, has been another approach, the delineation of the marks of the church. Since the destruction of the organizational unity of the Western church which occurred in the Protestant Reformation, this approach has been closely connected with the question concerning the essence of the true church.

Classically, theologians, building from the wording of the Apostles' Creed, have delineated the church's essence in terms of four characteristics or "marks"—apostolicity, catholicity, unity and holiness.[33] Although Protestants and Catholics enjoy basic agreement concerning these hallmarks, the two major church traditions view these terms quite differently.

Hendrickus Berkhof notes that beginning with the Counter-Reformation, the Roman Catholic church moved beyond the older view of the four marks as "normative points of orientation" and came to see them as "visible and tangible qualities, through which the true church distinguishes itself, for all to see, from the heretics."[34] Further, in the Roman Catholic tradition (and certain other church bodies that follow what might be termed a "high church" ecclesiology) apostolicity has focused on apostolic succession, understood as guaranteeing the perpetuity of the church. The true universal church, therefore, is that body whose bishops trace their ordination by means of apostolic succession to the first-century church. A local congregation, in turn, participates in the universal church insofar as it stands in fellowship with, or under the direction of, a bishop of the true church— a church leader whose ordination can be traced back through time to the apostles.

Because of their concern that a church could outwardly conform to the four marks but lack a vital relationship with Christ, the Reformers shifted the focus from the traditional marks to "Word and sacrament." Berkhof explains: "The pure preaching of the word and the right administration of the sacraments, in accordance with the Bible . . . would guarantee the bond with Christ, unobstructed by human devises."[35]

Although there are evangelicals among the advocates of each of these options, many thinkers in our movement opt for yet another alternative, which declares that the true church is essentially people standing in voluntary covenant with God. According to Robert T. Handy, the architects of this view argued that the church "was not parochial, diocesan, provincial, or national, but was congregational, gathered by an act of mutual confederation . . . expressed in a covenant."[36] As believers join together with the purpose of walking as God's people under Christ, the church exists.

The covenant concept enjoys an enviable biblical pedigree. At the heart of the scriptural concept of covenant is a fundamental pattern that Paul Hanson finds "underlying the community-building of God's people in every age": "the pattern of divine initiative and human response." Hanson adds, "This pattern comes to expression in the recurrent biblical formulation of covenant: 'I shall be your God, and you shall be my people.' "[37]

The move to covenant as the foundation of the church soon led to a radically new polity known as congregationalism. The newer ecclesiology brought several sharp differences from the older medieval and Reformation outlooks. One significant innovation lay in the congregationalist understanding of the soteriological relation between the believer and the church. Arguing that the church is formed through the covenant making of its members, congregationalists reversed the older order of the priority of the corporate over the individual. Rather than the individual Christian's being the product of the church, congregationalism claims that the church is formed by the coming together of believers. This means that in the order of salvation the believer, not the church, stands first.

Another innovation follows from the congregationalists' emphasis on the idea of the covenant, which they inherited as participants in the English Puritan movement. For the early congregationalists, the formation of the covenant meant that "discipline" must be added to "Word and sacrament" as essential to the true church. This inclusion of church discipline as a mark of the church, however, naturally led them to place an increased emphasis on the quest for church purity.

Perhaps the most radical innovation of congregationalism came in the area of the nature of the church. Certain congregationalist thinkers came to realize that the heightened emphasis on covenant as the church's foundation implied that the church exists only in local congregations.[38] Indeed, this radical turn to the visible church arose as a corollary of the covenant idea. If the church is constituted by the covenant, where there is no covenanting community—no body of believers uniting together into a local congregation—there is no church. And the covenant is by its very nature local, being the agreement among a particular, visible group of believers.[39]

Although the New Testament does not explicitly address the question of the marks of the church, the documents do present several pertinent themes. As we have seen, in the minds of the early Christians, believers themselves constitute the church. This understanding is evident in the term they chose to express their self-identity *(ekklēsia)*. It is prominent as well in much of the New Testament imagery of the church. Peter, for example, viewed the church as a temple made from individual "living stones" (1 Pet 2:5), and Paul saw the church as one body consisting of its individual members (1 Cor 12:12, 27).[40]

While emphasizing the people as a whole, the New Testament also sets forth the foundational role of leaders. Matthew and Acts explicitly emphasize the primacy of Peter and the significance of the twelve apostles. The Roman Catholic use of Matthew 16:15-19 to show that Jesus both installed Peter as the first among the apostles and established the perpetual primacy of the bishop of Rome is of course unwarranted. Nevertheless, this text is an indication that Jesus anticipated Peter's future role in the establishment of the infant church. Peter and the other apostles gave initial leadership to the Jerusalem community and spearheaded the proclamation of the gospel in the regions beyond the city.

The Pauline churches also accorded primacy to their leaders. Paul himself placed apostles and prophets at the head of the list of gifted persons

(1 Cor 12:27-28), although he was equally careful to balance this teaching with a parallel emphasis on the giftedness of all within the community. The epistle to the Ephesians summarizes the theme of leaders and their importance. For the purpose of edifying the whole body, Christ has given leaders to the church: apostles, prophets, evangelists and pastor-teachers (Eph 4:11-13). The Pauline emphasis on leaders reached its apex in the role of elders outlined in the pastoral epistles. Because of its importance, eldership is a worthy goal to which believers might aspire (1 Tim 3:1), and all would-be officeholders must pass stringent spiritual requirements (1 Tim 3:2-13).

The New Testament set the primacy of leaders within the context of an equal emphasis on servanthood and humility as the marks of true leadership. Leaders ought never to see their positions as a source of pride or an excuse for dominating others. Rather, they are called by God to serve the people (e.g., Mk 10:41-45). Leaders are to minister as shepherds and examples, never as overlords (1 Pet 5:1-5).

Covenant ecclesiology returns us to the concept of *ekklēsia*. Covenant means that ultimately the essence of the church lies with its people. But the *ekklēsia* is no ordinary collection of persons. Rather, because the church has been called out of the world by the preaching of the gospel in order to stand in covenant, it is constituted by people with a special consciousness. As J. M. R. Tillard notes, "This *koinonia* is not an assembly of friends. It is the coming together in Christ of men and women reconciled."[41]

Because its participants all confess allegiance to Christ, the community is conscious of its standing as a body under his lordship; it is a community in covenant with God through Christ. At the same time, the members' mutual confession of Christ means that they are conscious of their special standing in fellowship with each other; their shared commitment to be Christ's disciples entails a commitment to each other. The church-constituting covenant, therefore, is a mutual agreement to walk together as the people of God. And because of this mutual covenant, each member senses a responsibility to nurture the confession of Christ in all others through edification, encouragement and assistance. In short, because of Christ the church is a community of believers in covenant with God and with each other.

Despite the basic correctness of the congregationalist affirmation that the church is constituted by people who enter into covenant, we must not lose sight of the fact that the church transcends the totality of its members at any given time. Through the covenant we enter a fellowship that is already endowed with a history. This realization serves to relativize any assertion that the believer is logically prior to the church. Rather than focusing on the primacy of either, we must declare that the church and the believer are interdependent. Because the coming together of believers in mutual covenant constitutes it, the church is the covenant community of individuals. At the same time, through its proclamation of the gospel the church is instrumental in the process or inception of faith in those individuals who enter the covenant community. And that community enjoys a history and tradition transcending its present membership.

The Center of Ecclesiology

While helpful, these widely held ecclesiological points remain incomplete as the foundation for a revisioned doctrine of the church. If we are to set forth a renewing vision for our day, we cannot rely only on these images, as helpful as they are. As is indicated by the conclusions of the previous chapter, the integration of two additional points of departure—two themes that we can mine from the Scriptures, our heritage and contemporary thought—offer us assistance in our constructive project. Both of these motifs—kingdom and community—are related to the central Reformed theme of the covenant community.

If we were to point to one topic that above all others has inspired the labors of biblical scholars and theologians in the twentieth century, this topic would no doubt be the kingdom of God. Beginning with the profound discovery of Johannes Weiss late in the nineteenth century that Jesus' proclamation of the kingdom of God lay at the heart of his ministry, the greatest minds in New Testament studies and theology have wrestled with the nature and significance of this biblical theme. In fact, the resultant rise of kingdom theology has meant that any ecclesiology that purports to be biblical must now speak to the issue of the relationship of the church to the reign of God.[42]

Although the rediscovery of the kingdom of God is a late-nineteenth- and twentieth-century phenomenon, the relationship between the church and the kingdom is actually an old issue in theological history. Augustine wrestled with the question in his masterpiece, *City of God.* The Augustinian position, or perhaps a misunderstanding of it, formed the basis for the virtual equating of the earthly reality of the divine kingdom with the visible church, characteristic of the ecclesiology of the Middle Ages. Medieval Roman Catholicism suggested that a person's presence in the visible church was tantamount to being in the kingdom of God. This claim, coupled with the sacramental system and the right of excommunication, invested great power in the church hierarchy and clergy.

Protestants, in turn, tended to equate the kingdom with the invisible church, the spiritual body of Christ. Even in nineteenth-century liberal thinking the idea persisted, as theologians closely linked the kingdom of God with the disciples of Jesus, the recipients of the heightened God-consciousness or the society of people of good will.

But in the nineteenth and twentieth centuries a quite opposite response to the question of the relationship between the church and the kingdom took root in evangelical circles, due largely to the rising influence of dispensationalism. This theology introduced a rigid, even metaphysical, dichotomy between the kingdom—viewed as the future temporal, millennial rule of Messiah over all the earth—and the church. Classic dispensationalists argued that during the millennium prominence will be given to Israel, God's earthly people, whereas the church is the spiritual, heavenly people of God and the focal point of God's work in this present era. Like its Augustinian alternative, the dispensationalist disjunction is an oversimplification of what is in reality a complex relationship between the church and the kingdom. Nevertheless, by reintroducing the eschatological dimension to ecclesiology, dispensationalism has served an important purpose.

In the final analysis, we dare neither equate nor radically separate the church and the kingdom. Rather, the church is best seen as the *product* of the kingdom. As René Padilla notes, "The Church is not the Kingdom of God, but it is the concrete result of the Kingdom."[43] It is produced by the obedient response to Jesus' announcement of the reign of God. Consequently, it is to be an anticipatory expression and sign of God's reign.

Here we as evangelicals do well to learn from the Anabaptist tradition. According to the Mennonite scholar C. Norman Kraus, the early Anabaptists viewed the church as "the sphere of obedience to kingdom authority." For them it was "an authentic reflection of God's will 'on earth as it is in heaven' . . . the realm in which the 'peace, justice, and joy of the Holy Spirit' were experienced in this world."[44]

The church cannot simply be equated with the kingdom of God. The concept of the kingdom includes kingship—God's right to rule. Because this right is bound up with the prerogatives of God as Creator, the kingdom of God as God's inherent right is independent of the church's existence. Consequently, the kingdom preexists and is always broader in scope than the church. Further, *the kingdom of God* refers to God's domain in all its aspects, a domain that encompasses the entire created universe as well as the heavenly court. *Church,* in contrast, refers to God's program in calling out a people through Christ for his own. As such it is one dimension, albeit a central aspect, of the broader divine goal of establishing God's reign.

As a dimension of the program directed toward the reign of God, the church is dependent on the kingdom. This dependence arises from the fact that the church is the outgrowth of the message of the kingdom. God's right to rule declared and demonstrated by Jesus produces the church, for the proclamation of the message of Jesus' lordship evokes obedient human response, resulting in the building of the corporate community of faith. The church, in other words, is called forth by the proclamation of the message of the kingdom of God. Likewise, the church is dependent on the kingdom in that it is entrusted with the task of proclaiming the kingdom message and being the advance company of those who acknowledge the rule of God. The church is the eschatological community, declaring by word and deed the rule of God, which one day will be consummated and universal throughout the cosmos.

The link of the church to the reign of God means that ecclesiology has an unavoidable future reference. And this eschatological orientation ought to shape our understanding of the doctrine of the church. The people of God, the body of Christ, the temple of the Spirit is not called out merely to be an enclave of salvation or a ghetto of piety apart from or beyond the wickedness of the surrounding world. Rather, believers enter into covenant with God and each other in order that they might be "the eschatological community," the fellowship called into existence in order to pioneer in the present the principles that characterize the reign of God. They make up the church for the sake of the future of the world.

This eschatologically based understanding demands that we develop what we may term the "process model" of the church. Ultimately, our corporate life, like that of the individual Christian, is constituted by neither its past nor its present, but its future. What the church is, is determined by what the church is destined to become. And the church is directed toward the destiny God intends for humankind: participation in the consummated reign of God. This eschatological-process model forms a contrast to its neo-Platonic alternatives, which view the church as constituted by the heavenly archetype preexisting in God's mind.

Each of these two ecclesiologies carries implications for our understanding of the purpose of the church in the world. In neo-Platonic models, the goal of the church is to emulate its heavenly archetype. For example, some Calvinist ecclesiologies, building from the thesis that prior to the creation of the world God determined who would be the elect, assert that the mission of the church in history is to make visible the invisible company of the elect. Its mission, therefore, is to bring within its boundaries all the elect—all who were chosen by God in eternity past.

The eschatological-process alternative, in contrast, asserts that the church is constituted by its destiny as the company of the kingdom. The mission of the church, therefore, is not limited to bringing the elect into the fold. Rather, it includes the task of actualizing in the present—modeling for the world to see and as a sign of the eschatological reality—the glorious fellowship that will come in its fullness at the consummation of history. For this reason the church includes within its boundaries all who declare their allegiance to Jesus as Lord. And the church strives to be a prophetic voice in society, to proclaim by word and action what it means to live under the guidelines of the kingdom of God—love, peace, justice and righteousness.

The approach to ecclesiology that views the church in terms of the coming kingdom of God has gained broad support in recent years. Its newfound importance to Roman Catholic thinkers reached a high point in the Dogmatic Constitution on the Church developed by the Second Vatican Council, which describes the church as the "sign and sacrament" of the kingdom. Even Orthodox theologians now employ this idea. In describing Orthodox theology and liturgical practice, Petros Vassiliadis asserts that the church "does not draw her identity from what she is, or from what was given to her as an institution, but from what she will be, i.e., from the *eschata.*" Eschatology, therefore, "constitutes the primary aspect, the beginning of the Church." Consequently, the church "only prepares the way to the kingdom"—that is, the church is "an *eikon* of the kingdom to come."[45]

As helpful an advance over older approaches as the eschatological model of the church may be, it alone does not paint the complete picture. The focus on the church's relation to the kingdom leaves unanswered the question of the actual nature of the eschatological community God is seeking to bring to pass. Therefore, in developing a revisioned evangelical theology, we must add another perspective to those already cited. The church is the community of love, called to reflect the nature of the triune God.[46] Ultimately, therefore, our ecclesiology must take its point of departure from the relationship of the church to the reality of God. Hence the doctrine of God—theology proper—provides the final foundation for ecclesiology.

Evangelicals rightly affirm that God's program in the world is directed to individual humans in the midst of their sin and need. Unfortunately, this emphasis, correct as it is, has all too often resulted in an insufficient ecclesiology, reflecting a truncated soteriology, arising from a faulty theology. The church is far more than a collection of saved individuals who band together for the task of winning the lost, for the program of God moves beyond the salvation of the isolated individual. The divine program overflows the individual to encompass social interaction. And it moves beyond the isolated human realm to encompass all creation. God's concern is not merely to bring about the redeemed individual. Rather, he intends to bring forth a corporate, reconciled body, "one new humanity" (Eph 2:14-19), living in the redeemed new creation and enjoying the presence and fellowship of the Creator and Savior God.

This corporate-cosmic dimension of God's program reflects a complete biblical soteriology, which is related to the complete biblical picture of the nature of guilt and estrangement. We are guilty before God and estranged from God. But this guilt and estrangement are also experienced in our relationships with one another, with ourselves and with creation. Consequently, the salvific program of God is not only directed to establishing "peace with God"; it extends to the healing of all relationships—to ourselves, to one another and to nature.

God's interest in the creation of the reconciled community arises out of the divine nature itself. Reformed theology has traditionally focused on God's glory as the final rationale and goal for the work of creation and salvation. This is, of course, proper. However, the way theologians frame their understanding of the divine glory is often unhelpful. It so easily leaves us with the impression that God is a cosmic super-egotist demanding all praise and honor. In this way, God appears to be diametrically opposite from what the Bible sets forth as the ideal human character. How can God demand that in all our actions we remain humble, if God himself directs all his activities toward his own exaltation? In what sense could we ever fulfill the divine intention that we be the image of God?

God's glory may indeed be the final goal of all his actions. But if we are to understand it properly, this theme must be understood in a trinitarian sense—arising out of God's reality as the triune One, rather than as a solitary subject. Simply stated, God's salvific purposes are directed toward bringing God's highest creation—humankind—to reflect the eternal divine nature, that is, bringing us to be in actuality the image of God. And the image of God consists ultimately in love.

No theologian would deny that love is to be ranked among the greatest attributes of God. But we must take this affirmation further: love is a central, if not *the* central, attribute of God. It describes not only God in relationship to the world but also God in the divine eternal nature apart from the world. The Christian doctrine of the Trinity provides the key to understanding how this can be the case.

Love is a relational term, requiring both subject and object. (Someone loves someone else.) Were God a solitary acting subject, God would require the world as the object of his love, in order to be the Loving One. But the doctrine of the Trinity asserts that throughout eternity God is Father, Son and Holy Spirit. The divine reality encompasses a multiplicity within the Godhead. The classical formulation of the doctrine as espoused by Augustine moves a step further. The foundation for the triunity of God lies with the eternal love relation between the Father and the Son, a relation of love that is concretized in the third person, the Holy Spirit.[47] Throughout eternity, therefore, God is the community of love—Father, Son and Spirit distinct yet united through the love they share.

An important and far-reaching implication for ecclesiology follows from the affirmation that through all eternity God is the community of love. God's soteriological purposes are to bring glory to his own triune nature by establishing a reconciled creation in which humans reflect in relation to each other and to nature the reality of the Creator. As we exist in love, we reflect what God is like.

The primary vehicle for mirroring the divine image is the church. As the people united, we are called to exemplify in the midst of present brokenness the eschatological ideal community of love, which is the divine essence itself. In short, the church is to be the community of love, the fellowship of individuals who are bound together by the love present among them through the power of God's Spirit.

The mandate of the church extends to its members and binds all believers to each other and to the common whole. As persons, we are called to reflect the image of God—that is, to live in the pattern of the life of the triune God. But this exemplification of the image can only occur within the context of community—specifically, the community of the people who acknowledge the lordship of Jesus the Christ. We are dependent on the community of Christ in the task of reflecting the divine image, simply because the Christian community is the bearer of the self-revelation of the triune God. It is through the book of the community, the Bible, that we learn about and are brought into encounter with the life of the triune God. But further, because God is a social reality, it is only in relationship, in community, that we are able to reflect the divine nature.[48] And through its ongoing life, the community of believers under the direction of the Spirit through the Scriptures offers its members both the cognitive framework and practical instruction for the life of discipleship.

God has graciously brought us to participate together in the mystery of the triune life. Insofar as we participate in this community life, we are in the image of God. The community, therefore, is vital both for our understanding of our personal and corporate identity and for our growth in the life of discipleship.

But the community of love the church is called to be is no ordinary reality. Through conversion, the Holy Spirit causes us to be the children of God. This means that we are partakers of the love relationship shared between the Father and the Son. Consequently, the fellowship we share with each other is not merely a common experience or a common narrative, as important as these are. Our fellowship is nothing less than our common participation in the divine communion between the Father and the Son. Because of Christ's work on our behalf and the Spirit's work within us, we are coadoptees into the family of God, coparticipants in the relationship enjoyed between the Father and the Son which is the Holy Spirit. As Tillard rightly declares, "The ecclesial *koinonia* can be defined as the passing of the Trinitarian Communion into the fraternal relations of the disciples of Christ. . . . Seen from the human side, the ecclesial *koinonia* is none other than the fraternity of the disciples of Christ Jesus but in so far as it is caught up, seized by the Spirit who inserts it in the relation of the Father and the Son."[49]

From this primary identity, and only from this, can we ultimately derive the various other facets of our doctrine of the church. Our participation in the divine life forms the foundation for the mission of the church in the world. It constitutes the link between the church as a whole and its local, visible expressions. And it provides the foundation for the significance of the church as the covenant community. The Roman Catholic scholar Killian McDonnell rightly concludes concerning the ramifications of a turn to this concept of *communio* for our doctrine of the church, "No other category offers the possibility of an integral ecclesiology of such breadth and depth."[50]

To summarize: The triune God desires that human beings be brought together into a corporate whole, a fellowship of reconciliation, which not only reflects God's own eternal reality but actually participates in that reality. Since the New Testament era the focal point of the reconciled society in history has been the church of Jesus Christ, the new covenant people. As that people, we are called to pioneer in the present the community of love and thereby to participate in and reflect the eternal relation of the triune God, the community we will enjoy in the great eschatological fellowship on the renewed earth.

We are the company of those who already have been brought by the Holy Spirit to share in the love between the Father and the Son. When we are able to lay hold of and then articulate clearly this vision of the church, we may well gain a renewed sense of the presence of God within the Christian fellowship of love. And this in turn will spill over into a renewed worship "in spirit and in truth" as we praise the triune community of love, the eternal Trinity who is our Creator and Savior.

This glorious biblical vision of God's ultimate purpose for creation can fuel a revisioning of evangelical theology. John captured this vision in the closing chapters of the Apocalypse:

> Then I saw a new heaven and a new earth, for the first heaven and the first earth had passed away, and there was no longer any sea. I saw the Holy City, the new Jerusalem, coming down out of heaven from God, prepared as a bride beautifully dressed for her husband. And I heard a loud voice from the throne saying, "Now the dwelling of God is with men, and he will live with them. They will be his people, and God himself will be with them and be their God. He will wipe every tear from

their eyes. There will be no more death or mourning or crying or pain, for the old order of things has passed away."

He who was seated on the throne said, "I am making everything new!" (Rev 21:1-5)

Notes

Introduction

[1]Donald W. Dayton, "Some Doubts About the Usefulness of the Category 'Evangelical,' " in *The Variety of American Evangelicalism,* ed. Donald W. Dayton and Robert K. Johnston (Downers Grove, Ill.: InterVarsity Press, 1991), p. 251.

[2]Merold Westphal, "The Ostrich and the Boogeyman: Placing Postmodernism," *Christian Scholars Review* 20 (December 1990):15.

[3]Ted Peters, "Toward Postmodern Theology," *Dialog* 24 (Summer 1985):221.

[4]See, for example, Robert N. Bellah et al., *Habits of the Heart: Individualism and Commitment in American Life* (Berkeley: University of California Press, 1985), p. 65.

[5]Daniel A. Helminiak, "Human Solidarity and Collective Union in Christ," *Anglican Theological Review* 70 (January 1988):37.

Chapter 1: Revisioning Evangelical Identity

[1]Richard Quebedeaux, *The Worldly Evangelicals* (San Francisco: Harper & Row, 1978), p. 6.

[2]See, for example, Morris A. Inch, *The Evangelical Challenge* (Philadelphia: Westminster Press, 1978), p. 10; Donald G. Bloesch, *The Future of Evangelical Christianity* (Garden City, N.Y.: Doubleday, 1983), p. 15; Robert E. Webber, *Common Roots: A Call to Evangelical Maturity* (Grand Rapids, Mich.: Zondervan, 1978), pp. 25-27; Ronald H. Nash, *Evangelicals in America* (Nashville: Abingdon, 1987), p. 22. This point was also foundational to the section concerning evangelical identity in the document that arose from the 1989 consultation on Evangelical Affirmations co-sponsored by the National Association of Evangelicals and Trinity Evangelical Divinity School. See Kenneth S. Kantzer and Carl F. H. Henry, eds., *Evangelical Affirmations* (Grand Rapids, Mich.: Zondervan, 1990), p. 37.

[3]Billy Graham, preface to John D. Allan's *The Evangelicals: An Illustrated History* (Grand Rapids, Mich.: Baker Book House, 1989).

[4]For a summary of the recent literature, see Leonard I. Sweet, "The Evangelical Tradition in America," in *The Evangelical Tradition in America,* ed. Leonard I. Sweet (Macon, Ga.: Mercer University Press, 1984), pp. 1-86.

[5]In 1989, the World Evangelical Fellowship—a body seeking to be a "truly internationally representative meeting point for evangelicals of every kind"—commissioned a popular recounting of the rise of the movement. The volume, *The Evangelicals: An Illustrated History,* exemplifies the current tendency.

[6]The uncontested acceptance of this understanding is evidenced by its repeated employment in evangelical literature. Abraham, for example, states matter-of-

factly, "So the term 'evangelical' embraces at least three constellations of thought: the Reformation, led by Luther and Calvin, the evangelical revival of the eighteenth century as found, say, in Methodism, and modern conservative evangelicalism." William J. Abraham, *The Coming Great Revival* (San Francisco: Harper & Row, 1984), p. 73.

[7]Evangelical affinity with the Reformation is capsuled in a description offered as an introduction for persons joining the movement: "First and foremost evangelicals are people who believe in and live by the gospel of Jesus Christ as defined and articulated by the Protestant Reformers." William W. Wells, *Welcome to the Family: An Introduction to Evangelical Christianity* (Downers Grove, Ill.: InterVarsity, 1979), p. 129.

[8]Karl Barth, *The Humanity of God* (Atlanta: John Knox Press, 1960), p. 11. This definition is quoted by Inch, *The Evangelical Challenge*, p. 10.

[9]Donald W. Dayton, "The Limits of Evangelicalism," in *The Variety of American Evangelicalism,* ed. Donald W. Dayton and Robert K. Johnston (Downers Grove, Ill.: InterVarsity Press, 1991), p. 48.

[10]Wells, *Welcome to the Family,* p. 119.

[11]Dayton, "The Limits of Evangelicalism," p. 48.

[12]William G. McLoughlin, introduction to *The American Evangelicals, 1800-1900,* ed. William G. McLoughlin (New York: Harper Torchbooks, 1968), p. 1.

[13]Nash, *Evangelicals in America,* pp. 59-60. See also George M. Marsden, *The Evangelical Mind and the New School Presbyterian Experience* (New Haven, Conn.: Yale University Press, 1970), p. 244.

[14]For an early historical discussion of the five fundamentals, see Stewart Grant Cole, *The History of Fundamentalism* (New York: R. R. Smith, 1931), p. 34.

[15]George M. Marsden, *Fundamentalism and American Culture* (New York: Oxford University Press, 1980), p. 117.

[16]George M. Marsden, *Reforming Fundamentalism: Fuller Seminary and the New Evangelicalism* (Grand Rapids, Mich.: Eerdmans, 1987), p. 3.

[17]Daniel B. Stevick, *Beyond Fundamentalism* (Richmond, Va.: John Knox Press, 1964), p. 28. Significant early expressions of that protest included Harold John Ockenga's "Can Christians Win America?" which appeared in *Christian Life and Times,* June 1947, pp. 13-15. The author's answer to the query lodged in the title of the article was a resounding no. Fundamentalism was hampered by its divisive spirit, aloofness from social problems, and unethical practices, he asserted. The poignancy of Ockenga's short piece was echoed in the publication of a book-length critique, Carl F. H. Henry's *The Uneasy Conscience of Modern Fundamentalism* (Grand Rapids, Mich.: Eerdmans, 1947). Like Ockenga, Henry chastised his fellow fundamentalists for their aloofness from society and their lack of a social vision.

[18]For a presentation of the roots and rise of this movement, see Donald W. Dayton, *Theological Roots of Pentecostalism* (Grand Rapids, Mich.: Zondervan, 1987).

[19]C. Norman Kraus correctly describes evangelicalism as "a postfundamentalist coalition of conservative Protestant Christians who wished to return to the more centrist position of an earlier generation of conservative denominational theologians." C. Norman Kraus, "Evangelicalism: A Mennonite Critique," in *The Variety of American Evangelicalism*, ed. Donald W. Dayton and Robert K. Johnston (Downers Grove, Ill.: InterVarsity Press, 1991), p. 184.

[20]See George M. Marsden, "Defining Evangelicalism," in *Southern Baptists and American Evangelicals*, ed. David Dockery (Nashville: Broadman, 1993).

[21]George M. Marsden, ed., *Evangelicalism and Modern America* (Grand Rapids, Mich.: Eerdmans, 1984), xv.

[22]Russell L. Staples, "Adventism," in *The Variety of American Evangelicalism*, ed. Donald W. Dayton and Robert K. Johnston (Downers Grove, Ill.: InterVarsity Press, 1991), p. 67.

[23]For a discussion of these, see Millard Erickson, *The New Evangelical Theology* (Westwood, N.J.: Revell, 1968), pp. 31-44.

[24]Harold Lindsell, *The Battle for the Bible* (Grand Rapids, Mich.: Zondervan, 1976), p. 210.

[25]Francis A. Schaeffer, *The Great Evangelical Disaster* (Westchester, Ill.: Crossway Books, 1984), p. 64.

[26]Ibid., p. 57.

[27]David L. Edwards and John Stott, *Evangelical Essentials: A Liberal-Evangelical Dialogue* (Downers Grove, Ill.: InterVarsity Press, 1988).

[28]Clark H. Pinnock and Delwin Brown, *Theological Crossfire: An Evangelical-Liberal Dialogue* (Grand Rapids, Mich.: Zondervan, 1991).

[29]Donald G. Bloesch, *The Evangelical Renaissance* (Grand Rapids, Mich.: Eerdmans, 1973), pp. 48-79.

[30]Donald G. Bloesch, *Essentials of Evangelical Theology*, 2 vols. (San Francisco: Harper & Row, 1978-79).

[31]Ibid., 1:ix.

[32]Ibid., 1:5.

[33]Ibid., 2:276.

[34]James Davison Hunter, *Evangelicalism: The Coming Generation* (Chicago: University of Chicago Press, 1987), p. 19.

[35]Thomas Howard, *Evangelical Is Not Enough* (Nashville: Thomas Nelson, 1984), p. 5.

[36]David Parker, "Evangelical Spirituality Reviewed," *Colloquium* 23, no. 2 (1991):87.

[37]Howard, *Evangelical Is Not Enough*, p. 17.

[38]Ibid., p. 18.

[39]Bloesch, *The Future of Evangelical Christianity*, p. 108.

Chapter 2: Revisioning Evangelical Spirituality

[1]Lane Dennis, "A Call to Holistic Salvation," in *The Orthodox Evangelicals*, ed.

Robert E. Webber and Donald G. Bloesch (Nashville: Thomas Nelson, 1978), p. 95.

[2]Richard Quebedeaux, *The Worldly Evangelicals* (San Francisco: Harper & Row, 1978), pp. 22-23.

[3]This point is made by Douglas Jacobsen, "Re-visioning Evangelical Theology," *The Reformed Journal* 35 (October 1985):18-19.

[4]David L. McKenna, "Things of the Spirit, Matters of the Mind," *Christianity Today* 23 (February 16, 1979):27 [523].

[5]For a recent discussion, see David Parker, "Evangelical Spirituality Reviewed," *Evangelical Quarterly* 63, no. 2 (1991):123-46.

[6]William W. Wells, *Welcome to the Family: An Introduction to Evangelical Christianity* (Downers Grove, Ill.: InterVarsity Press, 1979), p. 10. Wells concludes the book with a slightly altered characterization, which substitutes interest in evangelism for the second mark (p. 182).

[7]Already in 1978 Richard Quebedeaux observed a constellation of changing attitudes among what he termed "the evangelical left," which included a shift away from the older emphasis on inerrancy and the propositional approach to the Bible to a more spirituality-oriented understanding. See Quebedeaux, *The Worldly Evangelicals,* pp. 98-99.

[8]This thesis is articulated by Sydney E. Ahlstrom, "From Puritanism to Evangelicalism: A Critical Perspective," in *The Evangelicals,* ed. David F. Wells and John D. Woodbridge, rev. ed. (Grand Rapids, Mich.: Baker Book House, 1977), p. 292.

[9]Drawing from Max Weber, Douglas Frank argues that in practical consequence Calvinism's doctrine of election led it to lapse into a doctrine of works. While this may have been the case on the popular level, it was, as Frank suggests, never set forth as Calvinist theology. See Douglas W. Frank, *Less Than Conquerors* (Grand Rapids, Mich.: Eerdmans, 1986), p. 130.

[10]For a short summary of Puritan spirituality, see James M. Houston, "Spirituality," in *The Evangelical Dictionary of Theology,* ed. Walter A. Elwell (Grand Rapids, Mich.: Baker Book House, 1984), pp. 1049-50.

[11]C. John Weborg, "Pietism: Theology in Service of Living Toward God," in *The Variety of American Evangelicalism,* ed. Donald W. Dayton and Robert K. Johnston (Downers Grove, Ill.: InterVarsity Press, 1991), p. 174.

[12]David Parker, "Evangelical Spirituality Reviewed," *Colloquium* 23, no. 2 (1991):85-91.

[13]Gordon S. Wakefield, "Spirituality," in *The Westminster Dictionary of Christian Theology,* ed. Alan Richardson and John Bowden (Philadelphia: Westminster Press, 1983), p. 549.

[14]Houston, "Spirituality," p. 1046.

[15]Robert E. Webber, *The Majestic Tapestry* (Nashville: Thomas Nelson, 1986), p. 114.

[16]For a somewhat similar delineation of these two themes, see ibid., pp. 115-17.

[17]Ernst Troeltsch, *The Social Teaching of the Christian Churches,* trans. Olive Wyon (New York: Harper Torchbooks, 1960), 2:993.

[18]See Timothy L. Smith, "The Cross Demands, the Spirit Enables," *Christianity Today* 23 (February 16, 1979):22-23 [518-19].

[19]David Parker, "Evangelical Spirituality Reviewed," *Colloquium* 23, no. 2(1991):86-87.

[20]For a discussion of the "victorious life movement" in the history of evangelicalism, see Frank, *Less Than Conquerors,* pp. 103-66.

[21]E.g., Donald G. Bloesch, *Essentials of Evangelical Theology* (San Francisco: Harper & Row, 1978-79), 2:257.

[22]Houston, "Spirituality," p. 1047.

[23]Ibid.

[24]Daniel B. Stevick, *Beyond Fundamentalism* (Richmond, Va.: John Knox Press, 1964), p. 127.

[25]Houston, "Spirituality," p. 1047.

[26]Ibid.

[27]Webber, *The Majestic Tapestry,* p. 129.

[28]This version of the Pietist adage is cited by Lesslie Newbigin, *The Gospel in a Pluralist Society* (Grand Rapids, Mich.: Eerdmans, 1989), p. 67.

[29]On this development, see Roch Kereszty, "Theology and Spirituality: The Task of a Synthesis," *Communio* 10 (Winter 1983):316-20.

[30]See Vernard Eller, "Which Eschatology for Which Christ?" *TSF Bulletin* 5 (November-December 1981):10.

[31]William J. Abraham, "Oh God, Poor God—The State of Contemporary Theology," *The Reformed Journal* 40 (February 1990):23.

[32]Houston, "Spirituality," p. 1047.

Chapter 3: Revisioning the Theological Task

[1]E.g., the statement produced by the 1989 consultation on Evangelical Affirmations cosponsored by the National Association of Evangelicals and Trinity Evangelical Divinity School as published in *Evangelical Affirmations,* ed. Kenneth S. Kantzer and Carl F. H. Henry (Grand Rapids, Mich.: Zondervan, 1990), pp. 37-38. See also Kenneth S. Kantzer, "Unity and Diversity in Evangelical Faith," in *The Evangelicals,* ed. David F. Wells and John D. Woodbridge, rev. ed. (Grand Rapids, Mich.: Baker Book House, 1977), pp. 59, 73.

[2]Klaus Bockmuehl, "The Task of Systematic Theology," in *Perspectives on Evangelical Theology,* ed. Kenneth S. Kantzer and Stanley N. Gundry (Grand Rapids, Mich.: Baker Book House, 1979), p. 4.

[3]For this latter point, see Frank Whaling, "The Development of the Word 'Theology,' " *Scottish Journal of Theology* 34 (1981):292-93.

[4]Emil Brunner, *The Christian Doctrine of God* (Philadelphia: Westminster Press, 1950), p. 89.

[5]Yves M. J. Congar, *A History of Theology* (Garden City, N.Y.: Doubleday, 1968), p. 33. See also G. R. Evans, *The Beginnings of Theology as an Academic Discipline* (Oxford: Clarendon, 1980).

[6]Whaling, "The Development of the Word 'Theology,' " p. 300.

[7]Edward Farley, *Theologia* (Philadelphia: Fortress, 1983), pp. 77, 81.

[8]Ibid., pp. 49, 65, 77.

[9]Whaling, "The Development of the Word 'Theology,' " pp. 305-6.

[10]See Brunner, *The Christian Doctrine of God*, pp. 93-96. Congar cites the church's need to speak to the pagan culture and the individual believer's need to reflect on faith in the pagan context. Congar, *A History of Theology*, pp. 39-40.

[11]This feature of evangelical theology is noted by David F. Wells, "An American Evangelical Theology: The Painful Transition from *Theoria* to *Praxis*," in *Evangelicalism and Modern America*, ed. George M. Marsden (Grand Rapids, Mich.: Eerdmans, 1984), p. 86.

[12]George M. Marsden, "Evangelical, History and Modernity," in *Evangelicalism and Modern America*, p. 98.

[13]Richard A. Muller, "Scholasticism Protestant and Catholic: Francis Turretin on the Object and Principles of Theology," *Church History* 55 (June 1986):204.

[14]Franciscus Turrettinus, *Institutio theologiae elencticae* (Geneva, 1677-85; rpt. Edinburgh, 1847), 1. 2. 6-7, as cited by Muller, "Scholasticism Protestant and Catholic," p. 204.

[15]Turrettinus *Institutio* 1. 5. 4; cited in Muller, "Scholasticism Protestant and Catholic," p. 200.

[16]Muller, "Scholasticism Protestant and Catholic," p. 205.

[17]Wells, "An American Evangelical Theology," p. 85.

[18]Charles Hodge, *Systematic Theology* (Grand Rapids, Mich.: Eerdmans, 1952), 1:18.

[19]George M. Marsden, *Fundamentalism and American Culture* (New York: Oxford University Press, 1980), p. 110.

[20]Wells, "An American Evangelical Theology," 85.

[21]Charles Hodge, *Princeton Sermons* (London: Banner of Truth Trust, 1958), p. xv.

[22]For an early statement of this theme, see Carl F. H. Henry, *The Protestant Dilemma: An Analysis of the Current Impasse in Theology* (Grand Rapids, Mich.: Eerdmans, 1949), p. 225.

[23]Carl F. H. Henry, *Frontiers in Modern Theology* (Chicago: Moody Press, 1966), pp. 134-35.

[24]Henry, *The Protestant Dilemma*, pp. 95-96.

[25]Ibid., p. 217.

[26]Carl F. H. Henry, *God, Revelation and Authority* (Waco, Tex.: Word Books, 1976-), 3:457.

[27]Ibid., 3:248-487.

[28]Henry, *The Protestant Dilemma*, p. 97.

[29]Henry, *God, Revelation and Authority,* 4:426.

[30]Ibid., 3:173.

[31]Henry, *The Protestant Dilemma,* p. 99.

[32]Carl F. H. Henry, *Remaking the Modern Mind* (Grand Rapids, Mich.: Eerdmans, 1946), p. 213.

[33]Henry, *God, Revelation and Authority,* 1:244.

[34]Ibid., 1:199.

[35]Carl F. H. Henry, "The Fortunes of Theology, Part 3," *Christianity Today* 16 (June 9, 1972):30 [874].

[36]Henry, *God, Revelation and Authority,* 1:215.

[37]Henry, *Remaking the Modern Mind,* 247.

[38]Henry, *God, Revelation and Authority,* 1:394.

[39]Ibid., 1:405; 2:136.

[40]Ibid., 2:83-85.

[41]For a lengthier discussion of this label and its significance in Henry's thought, see Bob E. Patterson, *Carl F. H. Henry* (Waco, Tex.: Word Books, 1983), pp. 58-83.

[42]Henry lays down the thesis that the Bible is the sole foundation for theology in *God, Revelation and Authority,* 1:181-409.

[43]See, for example, the characterization of John Baillie, *The Idea of Revelation in Recent Thought* (New York: Columbia University Press, 1956), p. 12.

[44]Ibid., pp. 27-40.

[45]See, for example, Millard J. Erickson, *Christian Theology* (Grand Rapids, Mich.: Baker Book House, 1983), 1:196.

[46]Ronald H. Nash, "Truth by Any Other Name," *Christianity Today* 22 (October 7, 1977):23.

[47]John Jefferson Davis, *Foundations of Evangelical Theology* (Grand Rapids, Mich.: Baker Book House, 1984), p. 67.

[48]See, for example, ibid., pp. 60-72.

[49]Erickson, *Christian Theology,* 1:21.

[50]Richard J. Gehman, "Guidelines in Contextualization," *East Africa Journal of Evangelical Theology* 2, no. 1 (1983):27.

[51]Clark H. Pinnock, *Tracking the Maze* (San Francisco: Harper & Row, 1990), p. 186.

[52]Ibid., pp. 183-84.

[53]Erickson, *Christian Theology,* 1:196.

[54]George A. Lindbeck, *The Nature of Doctrine* (Philadelphia: Westminster Press, 1984), p. 16.

[55]See, for example, Pinnock's statement on evangelical theological method. Clark H. Pinnock and Delwin Brown, *Theological Crossfire: An Evangelical-Liberal Dialogue* (Grand Rapids, Mich.: Zondervan, 1990), p. 45. This point is delineated in Lindbeck, *The Nature of Doctrine,* p. 80.

[56]Charles Taylor, *Sources of the Self: The Making of the Modern Identity* (Cambridge,

Mass.: Harvard University Press, 1989), pp. 25-40.

[57]For a sketch and appraisal of Luhmann's position, see Garrett Green, "The Sociology of Dogmatics: Niklas Luhmann's Challenge to Theology," *Journal of the American Academy of Religion* 50 (March 1982):19-34.

[58]Gerhard Sauter, *Wissenschaftstheoretische Kritik der Theologie* (Munich: Christian Kaiser, 1973), p. 330.

[59]Ronald F. Thiemann, "From Twilight to Darkness: Theology and the New Pluralism," *Trinity Seminary Review* 6 (Fall 1984):21.

[60]Peter Slater, "Theology in the 1990s," *Toronto Journal of Theology* 6 (Fall 1990):289.

[61]Theodore W. Jennings Jr., *Introduction to Theology* (Philadelphia: Fortress, 1976), p. 179.

[62]Lindbeck, *The Nature of Doctrine*, p. 18.

[63]See ibid., p. 33.

[64]See ibid., p. 80.

[65]For a discussion of this topic, see Colin Grant, "Dynamic Orthodoxy: A Polanyian Direction for Theology," *Studies in Religion* 17 (Fall 1988):412-15.

[66]Douglas F. Ottiti, "Christian Theology and Other Disciplines," *Journal of Religion* 64 (April 1984):182.

[67]Pinnock and Brown, *Theological Crossfire*, p. 161.

[68]James William McClendon, *Ethics*, vol. 1 of *Systematic Theology* (Nashville: Abingdon, 1986), p. 23.

[69]For a short discussion of the analogous nature of theology, see Davis, *Foundations of Evangelical Theology*, pp. 48-50.

[70]See, for example, Daniel B. Stevick, *Beyond Fundamentalism* (Richmond, Va.: John Knox Press, 1964), p. 69.

[71]Michael Goldberg, *Theology and Narrative* (Nashville: Abingdon, 1982), p. 95.

[72]Lindbeck, *The Nature of Doctrine*, p. 121.

Chapter 4: Revisioning the Sources for Theology

[1]See the Westminster Confession of Faith, 1.10, in *Creeds of the Churches: A Reader in Christian Doctrine from the Bible to the Present*, ed. John H. Leith, 3rd ed. (Atlanta: John Knox Press, 1982), p. 196.

[2]Paul Tillich, *Systematic Theology*, 3 vols. (Chicago: University of Chicago Press, 1951), 1:64.

[3]Clark H. Pinnock, *Tracking the Maze* (San Francisco: Harper & Row, 1990), p. 170-81.

[4]The genesis of the Wesleyan quadrilateral in the thinking of John Wesley has been rejected by Ted A. Campbell, "The 'Wesleyan Quadrilateral': The Story of a Modern Methodist Myth," *Methodist History* 29 (January 1991):87-95.

[5]For an exposition of the quadrilateral, see Donald A. D. Thorsen, *The Wesleyan Quadrilateral* (Grand Rapids, Mich.: Zondervan, 1990).

[6]Pinnock, *Tracking the Maze*, p. 171.

[7]Ibid., p. 179.

[8]Donald W. Dayton, "The Use of Scripture in the Wesleyan Tradition," in *The Use of the Bible in Theology: Evangelical Options*, ed. Robert K. Johnston (Atlanta: John Knox Press, 1985), p. 135.

[9]Paul Tillich, *Systematic Theology* (Chicago: University of Chicago Press, 1951), 1:42.

[10]For a lengthy discussion of theology as giving account of Christian faith, see Gerhard Ebeling, *Dogmatik des christlichen Glaubens* (Tübingen: J. C. B. Mohr [Paul Siebeck], 1982).

[11]Owen C. Thomas, "Theology and Experience," *Harvard Theological Review* 78, no. 1-2 (1985):192.

[12]Francis Schüssler Fiorenza, *Foundational Theology: Jesus and the Church* (New York: Crossroad, 1984), p. 259-64.

[13]Despite his rejection of experience as a source for theology, Owen C. Thomas nevertheless acknowledges this point. Thomas, "Theology and Experience," p. 197.

[14]For a similar delineation, see Gabriel Fackre, *The Christian Story* (Grand Rapids, Mich.: Eerdmans, 1984), p. 40.

[15]Karl Barth, *Church Dogmatics*, trans. G. W. Bromiley (Edinburgh: T. & T. Clark, 1975), 1(1):16.

[16]Robert E. Webber, *Common Roots: A Call to Evangelical Maturity* (Grand Rapids, Mich.: Zondervan, 1979), p. 139.

[17]Clark H. Pinnock, *The Scripture Principle* (San Francisco: Harper & Row, 1984), p. 217.

[18]Among evangelicals, Baptists have been an important voice in struggling with the problems surrounding creedalism. This denomination has generally stood against elevating any creed to binding authority.

[19]For one evangelical attempt to take seriously the contribution of culture, see Richard J. Gehman, "Guidelines in Contextualization," *East Africa Journal of Evangelical Theology* 2, no. 1 (1983):29-30.

[20]For a discussion of theological use and study of culture, see Robert J. Schreiter, *Constructing Local Theologies* (Maryknoll, N.Y.: Orbis Books, 1985), pp. 39-74.

[21]Ibid., p. 44.

[22]Webber, *Common Roots*, p. 139.

[23]John Calvin, *Defense Against Pighius*, as quoted in B. A. Gerrish, *Tradition and the Modern World* (Chicago: University of Chicago Press, 1977), p. 13.

[24]C. Norman Kraus, "A Mennonite Critique," in *The Variety of American Evangelicalism*, ed. Donald W. Dayton and Robert K. Johnston (Downers Grove, Ill.: InterVarsity Press, 1991), p. 197.

[25]Clark H. Pinnock and Delwin Brown, *Theological Crossfire: An Evangelical-Liberal Dialogue* (Grand Rapids, Mich.: Zondervan, 1990), p. 184.

Chapter 5: Revisioning Biblical Authority

[1]Mark A. Noll, *Between Faith and Criticism: Evangelicals, Scholarship and the Bible in America* (San Francisco: Harper & Row, 1986), p. 6.

[2]G. C. Berkouwer, *Holy Scripture* (Grand Rapids, Mich.: Eerdmans, 1975), p. 104.

[3]Dewey M. Beegle, *Scripture, Tradition and Infallibility* (Grand Rapids, Mich.: Eerdmans, 1973), p. 145.

[4]David Wright, review of James Barr's *Fundamentalism* in *Themelios* 3 (April 1978):88.

[5]Clark H. Pinnock, "What Is Biblical Inerrancy?" in *The Proceedings of the Conference on Biblical Inerrancy 1987* (Nashville: Broadman, 1987), p. 75.

[6]C. John Weborg, "Pietism: Theology in Service of Living Toward God," in *The Variety of American Evangelicalism*, ed. Donald W. Dayton and Robert K. Johnston (Downers Grove, Ill.: InterVarsity Press, 1991), pp. 170-71, 176.

[7]Ibid., p. 176.

[8]Michael Hardin, "The Authority of Scripture: A Pietist Perspective," *Covenant Quarterly* 49 (February 1991):9.

[9]Mary Ford, "Seeing, But Not Perceiving: Crisis and Context in Biblical Studies," *St. Vladimir's Theological Quarterly* 35, no. 2-3 (1991):122.

[10]Ibid., p. 124.

[11]Bernard Ramm, *The Pattern of Religious Authority* (Grand Rapids, Mich.: Eerdmans, 1959), p. 28.

[12]The Westminster Confession of Faith, 1.10, in *Creeds of the Churches: A Reader in Christian Doctrine from the Bible to the Present*, ed. John H. Leith, 3rd ed. (Atlanta: John Knox Press, 1982), p. 196.

[13]See H. D. McDonald, *An Historical Study: Ideas of Revelation 1700-1860* (London: Macmillan, 1959), pp. 266-88.

[14]The English Calvinist Baptists, for example, apparently did not follow the general Reformed pattern until after the composing of the Westminster Confession.

[15]For an example, note the table of contents in Millard J. Erickson, *Christian Theology* (Grand Rapids, Mich.: Baker Book House, 1983), 1:8-9. See also Harold Lindsell, "Inspiration," in *Zondervan Pictorial Encyclopedia of the Bible*, ed. Merrill C. Tenney (Grand Rapids, Mich.: Zondervan, 1976), 3:289.

[16]This position is indicative even of much of the so-called evangelical left. See, for example, David Allan Hubbard, *What We Evangelicals Believe* (Pasadena, Calif.: Fuller Theological Seminary, 1979), pp. 44-49.

[17]For an example, see James I. Packer, *"Fundamentalism" and the Word of God* (Grand Rapids, Mich.: Eerdmans, 1958), pp. 80-81. See also Robert P. Lightner, *Evangelical Theology* (Grand Rapids, Mich.: Baker Book House, 1986), p. 13.

[18]See the characterization of the traditional understanding by Thomas A. Hoffman, "Inspiration, Normativeness, Canonicity and the Unique Sacred Character of the Bible," *Catholic Biblical Quarterly* 44 (1982):453. For a recent reaffirmation of the classical view in an updated form, see James M. Reese, "Inspiration: Toward a

Sociosemiotic Definition," *Biblical Theology Bulletin* 21 (Spring 1991):10.

[19]Clark H. Pinnock, *The Scripture Principle* (San Francisco: Harper & Row, 1984), p. 13.

[20]For a summary of these alternatives, see Francis Schüssler Fiorenza, "The Crisis of Scriptural Authority: Interpretation and Reception," *Interpretation* 44 (October 1990):353-68.

[21]E.g., Stephen Reid, "An Evangelical Approach to Scripture," *TSF Bulletin* 8 (March-April 1985):2-10.

[22]Brevard Childs, *Introduction to the Old Testament as Scripture* (Philadelphia: Fortress, 1979), p. 60.

[23]Ibid., p. 74.

[24]Brevard Childs, *Biblical Theology in Crisis* (Philadelphia: Westminster Press, 1970), p. 141.

[25]Ibid., p. 104.

[26]Ibid., p. 105.

[27]Avery Dulles, "Scripture: Recent Protestant and Catholic Views," in *The Authoritative Word*, ed. Donald K. McKim (Grand Rapids, Mich.: Eerdmans, 1983), p. 246.

[28]David Kelsey, *The Uses of Scripture in Recent Theology* (Philadelphia: Westminster Press, 1975). For a subsequent statement, see David Kelsey, "The Bible and Christian Theology," *Journal of the American Academy of Religion* 48 (1980):385-402.

[29]E.g., John B. Rogers Jr., "The Book That Reads Us," *Interpretation* 39 (October 1985):388-401.

[30]Hoffman, "Inspiration, Normativeness, Canonicity," pp. 447-69.

[31]Edgar V. McKnight, "Errantry and Inerrancy: Baptists and the Bible," *Perspectives in Religious Studies* 12 (Summer 1985):146.

[32]Edward W. Goodrick, "Let's Put 2 Timothy 3:16 Back into the Bible," *Journal of the Evangelical Theological Society* 25 (December 1982):479-87.

[33]Ibid., pp. 486-87.

[34]Hoffman, "Inspiration, Normativeness, Canonicity," p. 457.

[35]For a critique of the extension of the "prophetic model" to all of Scripture, see Paul J. Achtemeier, *The Inspiration of Scripture* (Philadelphia: Westminster Press, 1980), pp. 99-104.

[36]Ibid., p. 92.

[37]Ibid., p. 116.

[38]Dulles, "Scripture," p. 250.

[39]Ibid., p. 260.

[40]Ibid., p. 250.

[41]Pinnock, *The Scripture Principle*, p. 217.

[42]Donald G. Bloesch, "In Defense of Biblical Authority," *The Reformed Journal* 34 (September 1984):30.

[43]Fiorenza, "The Crisis of Scriptural Authority," p. 363.

[44]Cf. John Howard Yoder, "The Use of the Bible in Theology," in *The Use of the Bible in Theology*, ed. Robert K. Johnston (Atlanta: John Knox Press, 1985), pp. 103-20.

[45]David H. Kelsey, *The Uses of Scripture in Recent Theology* (Philadelphia: Fortress, 1975), p. 89.

[46]Ibid., p. 214.

[47]For a somewhat similar idea, see James Barr, *The Scope and Authority of the Bible* (Philadelphia: Westminster Press, 1980), pp. 126-27.

[48]William R. Herzog II, "Interpretation as Discovery and Creation: Sociological Dimensions of Biblical Hermeneutics," *American Baptist Quarterly* 2 (June 1983):116.

[49]Barr, *The Scope and Authority of the Bible*, p. 36.

[50]Bernard Ramm has offered a service in raising Barth's banner within evangelicalism.

[51]Karl Barth, *Church Dogmatics*, trans. G. W. Bromiley, 2nd ed. (Edinburgh: T. & T. Clark, 1975), 1(1):88-124.

[52]G. C. Berkouwer, *Holy Scripture* (Grand Rapids, Mich.: Eerdmans, 1975), p. 166.

[53]Beegle, "Scripture, Tradition and Infallibility," pp. 19-21.

[54]Traugott Holz, "Apokalupsis," in *Exegetical Dictionary of the New Testament*, ed. Horst Balz and Gerhard Schneider (Grand Rapids, Mich.: Eerdmans, 1990), 1:132.

[55]See, for example, John Goldingay, *Approaches to Old Testament Interpretation* (Downers Grove, Ill.: InterVarsity Press, 1981), pp. 74-77; see also Packer, *"Fundamentalism" and the Word of God*, p. 92; George Eldon Ladd, "Revelation, History and the Bible," *Christianity Today* 1 (September 30, 1957):7; Daniel B. Stevick, *Beyond Fundamentalism* (Richmond, Va.: John Knox Press, 1964), pp. 104-6. For the neo-orthodox position, see John Baillie, *The Idea of Revelation in Recent Thought* (New York: Columbia University Press, 1956), pp. 62-65.

[56]See, for example, Richard J. Coleman, *Issues of Theological Conflict* (Grand Rapids, Mich.: Eerdmans, 1980), pp. 109-10.

[57]This tendency has been criticized by William J. Abraham, *The Divine Inspiration of Holy Scripture* (Oxford: Oxford University Press, 1981).

[58]Paul Rainbow, "On Hearing the Word of God," convocation address at North American Baptist Seminary, Sioux Falls, S.D., 1990.

[59]Ibid., p. 14.

[60]Donald G. Bloesch, *The Future of Evangelical Christianity* (Garden City, N.Y.: Doubleday, 1983), p. 118.

[61]Barr, *The Scope and Authority of the Bible*, p. 16; Beegle, *Scripture, Tradition and Infallibility*, pp. 307-8.

[62]Bloesch, *The Future of Evangelical Christianity*, p. 118.

[63]This theme is developed in Berkouwer, *Holy Scripture*, pp. 195-212.

[64]The charge of idolizing the Bible dies hard. It was repeated as late as 1982. See Sallie McFague, *Metaphorical Theology* (Philadelphia: Fortress, 1982), p. 4.

[65]John Baillie, *The Idea of Revelation in Recent Thought* (New York: Columbia University Press, 1956), p. 117.

[66]H. N. Ridderbos, "The Inspiration and Authority of Holy Scripture," in *The Authoritative Word,* ed. Donald K. McKim (Grand Rapids, Mich.: Eerdmans, 1983), p. 186.

Chapter 6: Revisioning Theology's Integrative Motif

[1]See, for example, Gerhard Sauter and Alex Stock, *Arbeitswesen Systematischer Theologie: Eine Anleitung* (Munich: Kaiser, 1976), pp. 18-19.

[2]This theme is proposed by Randy L. Maddox, "Responsible Grace: The Systematic Perspective of Wesleyan Theology," *Wesleyan Theological Journal* 19 (Fall 1984):12-18.

[3]Lewis Sperry Chafer, *Systematic Theology,* 8 vols. (Dallas: Dallas Seminary Press, 1947-48).

[4]Millard J. Erickson, *Christian Theology,* 3 vols. (Grand Rapids, Mich.: Baker Book House, 1983-85).

[5]Marjorie Hewitt Suchocki, *God, Christ, Church* (New York: Crossroad, 1984). See also John Cobb Jr., *A Christian Natural Theology* (Philadelphia: Westminster Press, 1965).

[6]James H. Cone, *A Black Theology of Liberation* (Philadelphia: J. B. Lippincott, 1970).

[7]Gustavo Gutierrez, *A Theology of Liberation* (Maryknoll, N.Y.: Orbis Books, 1980).

[8]See, for example, Rosemary Radford Ruether, *Sexism and God-Talk* (Boston: Beacon, 1983).

[9]George W. Stroup, *The Promise of Narrative Theology* (Atlanta: John Knox Press, 1973). See also Michael Goldberg, *Theology and Narrative* (Nashville: Abingdon, 1982), and Gabriel Fackre, *The Christian Story* (Grand Rapids, Mich.: Eerdmans, 1984).

[10]As an example of the widespread influence of this concept, see the published doctrinal dissertation of the general secretary of the World Council of Churches. Emilio Castro, *Freedom in Mission: The Perspectives of the Kingdom of God—An Ecumenical Inquiry* (Geneva: World Council of Churches, 1985).

[11]Ritschl's formal definition of the Kingdom of God is rather lengthy and complicated: "The uninterrupted reciprocation of action springing from the motive of love—a kingdom in which all are knit together in union with every one who can show the marks of a neighbour; further it is that union of men in which all goods are appropriated in their proper subordination to the highest good." Albrecht Ritschl, *The Christian Doctrine of Justification and Reconciliation* (Clifton, N.J.: Reference Books Publishers, 1966), pp. 334-35.

[12]Ibid., p. 282. Here Ritschl refers to the kingdom of God as God's own glory and personal end.

[13]Adolf Harnack, *What Is Christianity?* trans. Thomas Bailey Saunders (New York:

G. P. Putnam's Sons, 1901), pp. 216-20.

[14]Ibid., p. 122.

[15]For a short summary of the social gospel movement, see William E. Hordern, *A Layman's Guide to Protestant Theology*, rev. ed. (New York: Macmillan, 1968), pp. 85-86.

[16]Walter Rauschenbusch, *Christianity and the Social Crisis* (New York: Macmillan, 1907), p. xi.

[17]Johannes Weiss, *Jesus' Proclamation of the Kingdom of God*, trans. Richard H. Hiers and David L. Holland (Philadelphia: Fortress, 1971), p. 72.

[18]C. H. Dodd, *The Parables of the Kingdom* (London: Nisbett, 1935), p. 44.

[19]E.g., Anthony Hoekema, *The Bible and the Future* (Grand Rapids, Mich.: Eerdmans, 1979).

[20]E.g., Craig A. Blaising and Darrell L. Bock, eds., *Dispensationalism, Israel and the Church* (Grand Rapids, Mich.: Zondervan, 1992).

[21]For a fuller discussion of this development, see Stanley J. Grenz, *The Millennial Maze* (Downers Grove, Ill.: InterVarsity Press, 1992).

[22]Marcus J. Berg, "Jesus and the Kingdom of God," *Christian Century* 102 (April 22, 1987):378-80.

[23]Bruce D. Chilton, *God in Strength: Jesus' Announcement of the Kingdom* (Freistadt, Germany: Verlag F. Plöchl, 1978), pp. 287-88.

[24]Bruce D. Chilton, introduction to *The Kingdom of God in the Teachings of Jesus*, ed. Bruce D. Chilton, Issues in Religion and Theology 5 (Philadelphia: Fortress, 1984), p. 25.

[25]See Joel Marcus, "Entering into the Kingly Power of God," *Journal of Biblical Literature* 107, no. 4 (1988):663-75.

[26]Ibid., p. 674.

[27]In the 1960s J. Moltmann and W. Pannenberg were influential in focusing attention on the importance of the concept of the kingdom of God. See Jürgen Moltmann, *Theology of Hope* (New York: Harper & Row, 1965); Wolfhart Pannenberg, *Theology and the Kingdom of God* (Philadelphia: Westminster Press, 1969).

[28]For a response, see Mortimer Arias, *Announcing the Reign of God* (Philadelphia: Fortress, 1984), esp. p. xvi.

[29]See, for example, Robert N. Bellah et al., *Habits of the Heart: Individualism and Commitment in American Life* (Berkeley: University of California Press, 1985), p. 65.

[30]Ibid., p. 82.

[31]Ibid., p. 154.

[32]Ibid., pp. 152-53.

[33]Leonard I. Sweet, "The 1960s: The Crisis of Liberal Christianity and the Public Emergence of Evangelicalism," in *Evangelicalism and Modern America*, ed. George M. Marsden (Grand Rapids, Mich.: Eerdmans, 1984), p. 43.

[34]For a helpful summary, see L. Gregory Jones, "Why There Is No One Debate

Between 'Communitarians' and 'Liberals': An Essay on the Importance of Community," *Perspectives in Religious Studies* 17 (Spring 1990):53-70.

[35]Daniel A. Helminiak, "Human Solidarity and Collective Union in Christ," *Anglican Theological Review* 70 (January 1988):37.

[36]*Culturalism* is the term preferred by critic of the movement Robert J. McShea, *Morality and Human Nature: A New Route to Ethical Theory* (Philadelphia: Temple University Press, 1990), pp. 89-148.

[37]For a summary of the phenomenological analyses of human solidarity, see Helminiak, "Human Solidarity and Collective Union," pp. 37-44.

[38]For a recent summary of the importance of Royce, see Frank M. Oppenheim, "A Roycean Response to the Challenge of Individualism," in *Beyond Individualism: Toward a Retrieval of Moral Discourse in America*, ed. Donald L. Gelpi (Notre Dame, Ind.: University of Notre Dame Press, 1989), pp. 87-119.

[39]For a short overview, see "Josiah Royce," in *Dictionary of Philosophy and Religion*, ed. William L. Reese (Atlantic Highlands, N.J.: Humanities Press, 1980), pp. 498-99.

[40]Emile Durkheim, *The Division of Labor in Society*, trans. George Simpson (New York: Macmillan, 1964), p. 277.

[41]George Herbert Mead, *Mind, Self and Society*, ed. Charles W. Morris (1934; reprint ed. Chicago: University of Chicago Press, 1974), p. 123.

[42]For Mead's argument, see ibid., pp. 138-58.

[43]Bellah et al., *Habits of the Heart*, p. 84.

[44]This opinion was recently articulated by George A. Lindbeck, "Confession and Community: An Israel-like View of the Church," *Christian Century* 107 (May 9, 1990):495.

[45]Bellah et al., *Habits of the Heart*, p. 81.

[46]See, for example, Alisdair MacIntyre, *After Virtue*, 2nd ed. (Notre Dame, Ind.: University of Notre Dame Press, 1984), p. 221.

[47]E.g., Lindbeck, "Confession and Community," p. 495.

[48]Bellah et al., *Habits of the Heart*, pp. 81-82.

[49]Ibid., p. 282.

[50]Ibid., p. 72.

[51]Ibid., p. 134.

[52]Ibid., p. 333.

[53]Ibid., pp. 152-55.

[54]Ibid., p. 282.

[55]Ibid., pp. 152-54.

[56]For a discussion of the significance of this incident, see Edmund P. Clowney, "The Biblical Theology of the Church," in *The Church in the Bible and the World*, ed. D. A. Carson (Grand Rapids, Mich.: Baker Book House, 1987), pp. 25-26.

[57]Paul D. Hanson, *The People Called* (San Francisco: Harper & Row, 1986), p. 510.

[58]See, for example, James William McClendon, *Ethics*, vol. 1 of *Systematic Theology* (Nashville: Abingdon, 1986), 1:212-19.

[59]Hanson, *The People Called*, p. 537.

[60]For the development of this idea, see, for example, L. Gregory Jones, *Transformed Judgment: Toward a Trinitarian Account of the Moral Life* (Notre Dame, Ind.: University of Notre Dame Press, 1990), pp. 137-39.

[61]Peter C. Hodgson, "Ecclesia of Freedom," *Theology Today* 44 (April 1987):226.

Chapter 7: Revisioning the Church

[1]Andrew Kuyvenhoven, "Denominationalism: From Fanaticism to Indifference," *Faith Today* 9 (July-August 1991):13.

[2]E.g., Donald G. Bloesch, *The Evangelical Renaissance* (Grand Rapids, Mich.: Eerdmans, 1973), p. 41.

[3]Donald A. Carson, "Evangelicals, Ecumenism and the Church," in *Evangelical Affirmations*, ed. Kenneth S. Kantzer and Carl F. H. Henry (Grand Rapids, Mich.: Zondervan, 1990), p. 355.

[4]Ibid., p. 357.

[5]Clark H. Pinnock and Delwin Brown, *Theological Crossfire: An Evangelical-Liberal Dialogue* (Grand Rapids, Mich.: Zondervan, 1990), p. 198.

[6]Nathan O. Hatch, "Response to Carl F. H. Henry," in *Evangelical Affirmations*, pp. 98-99.

[7]Melvin Tinker, "Towards an Evangelical Ecclesiology," *Churchman* 105, no. 1 (1991):19.

[8]See, for example, John E. Toews, "The Nature of the Church," *Direction* 18 (Fall 1989):3-5; Marvin Hein, "Retrieving the Conference 'Glue,' " *Direction* 11 (July 1982):12-13.

[9]See, for example, Avery Dulles, "A Half Century of Ecclesiology," *Theological Studies* 50 (1989):419-42.

[10]Robert N. Bellah et al., *Habits of the Heart: Individualism and Commitment in American Life* (Berkeley: University of California Press, 1985), p. 226.

[11]Donald G. Bloesch, *The Future of Evangelical Christianity* (Garden City, N.Y.: Doubleday, 1983), p. 127.

[12]For an example see Dale Moody, *The Word of Truth* (Grand Rapids, Mich.: Eerdmans, 1981), pp. 427-33.

[13]For examples of the combination of these motifs, see Tinker, "Towards an Evangelical Ecclesiology," pp. 20-27; Donald Allister, "Ecclesiology: A Reformed Understanding of the Church," *Churchman* 103, no. 3 (1989):250-52. For a biblical study that combines *ekklēsia* with several New Testament metaphors for the church, see P. T. O'Brien, "The Church as a Heavenly and Eschatological Entity," in *The Church in the Bible and the World*, ed. D. A. Carson (Grand Rapids, Mich.: Baker Book House, 1987), pp. 88-119.

[14]E.g., Millard J. Erickson, *Christian Theology* (Grand Rapids, Mich.: Baker Book House, 1983-85), 3:1031. See also Robert P. Lightner, *Evangelical Theology* (Grand Rapids, Mich.: Baker Book House, 1986), pp. 227-28.

[15]Paul D. Hanson, *The People Called* (San Francisco: Harper & Row, 1986), p. 467.

[16]For the development of the biblical basis for an ecclesiology of the people of God, see George J. Brooke, "Laos: A Biblical Perspective for a Theology of 'The People of God,' " *Modern Churchman* 32, no. 3 (1990):32-40.

[17]*Baptism, Eucharist and Ministry,* Faith and Order Paper 111 (Geneva: World Council of Churches, 1982), p. 20.

[18]According to Kenneth Cauthen, *Systematic Theology* (Lewiston, N.Y.: Edwin Mellon, 1986), p. 296, the implicit trinitarianism of the choice of these metaphors and their significance as the three major motifs in the history of Christian thought dates to Lesslie Newbigin's book *The Household of Faith* (New York: Friendship, 1954). Millard Erickson, who employs them in his ecclesiology *(Christian Theology,* 3:1034-41), cites as the source of the idea Arthur W. Wainwright, *The Trinity in the New Testament* (London: SPCK, 1962).

[19]For a short discussion of the idea of priesthood, see Alex T. M. Cheung, "The Priest as the Redeemed Man: A Biblical-Theological Study of the Priesthood," *Journal of the Evangelical Theological Society* 29 (September 1986):265-75.

[20]*Baptism, Eucharist and Ministry,* p. 23. Historically, rather than being an occasion for the demonstration of unity, ecclesiology or the doctrine of the church has been a source of contention among Christians. Fortunately, the twentieth century has witnessed a reversal of the earlier trend. During the last decades thinkers from various denominations have reached something of a consensus concerning certain aspects of ecclesiology.

Already in 1958 Walter Marshall Horton noted broad agreement on six important points: The origin of the church lies in God's calling of a people in the Old Testament era. Nevertheless, the decisive formative act was the death and resurrection of Christ. The church is the community of the Holy Spirit. Although it is therefore a divine community, the church is also a human community. The church is related to the kingdom of God, but is not identical with it. And finally, the church has been given a mission in the world as well as an established ministry and appropriate means of grace to carry out its mission.

Despite broad agreement on these points, Horton noted four yet unresolved issues: Where is the true church and what are its boundaries? What is the correct form for organizing the church? How is the continuity of the church to be preserved (i.e., continuity of institutional authority or continuity of faith and message)? And what is the fundamental nature of the church (objective-corporate or subjective-individual)? Walter Marshal Horton, *Christian Theology: An Ecumenical Approach* (New York: Harper & Brothers, 1958), pp. 202-43.

[21]For a summary of the recent discussion concerning the body motif, see Andrew

Perriman, " 'His Body Which Is the Church . . .': Coming to Terms with Metaphor," *Evangelical Quarterly* 62, no. 2 (1990):123-42.

[22]See, for example, Augustus Hopkins Strong, *Systematic Theology* (Philadelphia: Griffith & Rowland, 1909), 3:887-91.

[23]Carson, "Evangelicals, Ecumenism and the Church," p. 367.

[24]Allan Janssen, "The Local God," *Perspectives* 6 (May 1991):14-16.

[25]See, for example, the conclusion of Karl L. Schmidt, "Ecclesia," in *Theological Dictionary of the New Testament,* ed. Gerhard Kittel and Gerhard Friedrich, trans. Geoffrey W. Bromiley (Grand Rapids, Mich.: Eerdmans, 1964-76), 3:504, 535.

[26]Klaas Runia, *Reformation Today* (London: Banner of Truth Trust, 1968), 33-34. Runia cites W. Stanford Reid, "Evangelical Defeat by Default," *Christianity Today* 6 (January 5, 1962): 28 [332].

[27]Lightner, *Evangelical Theology,* p. 228.

[28]Ibid., p. 232.

[29]Michael D. Williams, "Where's the Church? The Church as the Unfinished Business of Dispensational Theology," *Grace Theological Journal* 10, no. 2 (1989):167.

[30]C. Norman Kraus, "Anabaptism and Evangelicalism," in *Evangelicalism and Anabaptism,* ed. C. Norman Kraus (Scottdale, Pa.: Herald, 1979), pp. 177-78.

[31]Pinnock and Brown, *Theological Crossfire,* p. 148. Despite Pinnock's critique of evangelical ecclesiology, the book does little to foster a renewal of interest in this matter, for it contains no separate section on the doctrine of the church.

[32]Bloesch, *The Future of Evangelical Christianity,* p. 129.

[33]Recently several evangelical theologians have called for a return to the four traditional marks of the church. See, for example, Robert E. Webber, *Common Roots: A Call to Evangelical Maturity* (Grand Rapids, Mich.: Zondervan, 1979), pp. 55-71; Bloesch, *The Future of Evangelical Theology,* p. 127.

[34]Hendrickus Berkhof, *Christian Faith,* trans. Sierd Woudstra (Grand Rapids, Mich.: Eerdmans, 1979), pp. 409-10.

[35]Ibid., p. 409.

[36]Robert Theodore Handy, "The Philadelphia Tradition," in *Baptist Concepts of the Church,* ed. Winthrop Still Hudson (Philadelphia: Judson, 1959), p. 36.

[37]Hanson, *The People Called,* p. 469.

[38]As a result of and an impetus to this emphasis on the local congregation, the New Hampshire Confession of Faith omitted any reference to the concept of the universal church. The significance of this is noted by Winthrop Still Hudson, "By Way of Perspective," in *Baptist Concepts of the Church,* p. 27.

[39]The covenant-based ecclesiology of the Puritans led the early English Baptists to a radical position concerning the initiatory sacrament. From their reading of the New Testament, the Baptists concluded that baptism is the covenant that joins believers in the fellowship of Jesus Christ. But this meant that the covenant mark can be for believers only; it is simply impossible for individuals to express their

personal covenant with God and with the baptizing community through infant baptism.

[40]The New Testament emphasis on the church's being constituted by people must not be confused with the individualism that apparently gained strength in Baptist circles with the teachings of Francis Wayland, who conceived of the church as an aggregate of saved individuals. Norman H. Maring, "The Individualism of Francis Wayland," in *Baptist Concepts of the Church*, p. 147. The first-century Christians, in contrast, understood themselves as individually members of the corporate whole. Hence their ecclesiology exhibited a healthy balance between the individual and the group.

[41]J. M. R. Tillard, "What Is the Church of God?" *Mid-stream* 23 (October 1984):367.

[42]Hence Erickson, for example, lists the relationship between the church and the kingdom as the first of four special problems or "special areas which require particular attention in our introductory chapter on the doctrine of the church" (*Christian Theology*, 3:1041).

[43]C. René Padilla, "The Mission of the Church in the Light of the Kingdom of God," *Transformation* 1 (April-June 1984):17.

[44]C. Norman Kraus, "A Mennonite Critique," in *The Variety of American Evangelicalism*, ed. Donald W. Dayton and Robert K. Johnston (Downers Grove, Ill.: InterVarsity Press, 1991), pp. 191-92.

[45]Petros Vassiliadis, "Orthodox Theology Facing the Twenty-first Century," *Greek Orthodox Theological Review* 35, no. 2 (1990):149-50.

[46]Although not yet prominent, this theme has been the subject of a few preliminary explorations in recent years. For an example of a discussion from a free church perspective, see Miroslav Volf, "Kirche als Gemeinschaft: Ekklesiologische Überlegungen aus freikirchlicher Perspektive," *Evangelische Theologie* 49, no. 1 (1989):70-76. Roman Catholic ecclesiology has been moving in this direction as well. See, for example, Kilian McDonnell, "Vatican II (1962-1964), Puebla (1979), Synod (1985): *Koinonia/Communio* as an Integral Ecclesiology," *Journal of Ecumenical Studies* 25 (Summer 1988):414.

[47]Augustine *On the Trinity* 15. 17. 27-29, 31; 15. 19. 37.

[48]For a discussion of the implications of the social Trinity for the concept of the image of God, see Cornelius Plantinga Jr., "Images of God," in *Christian Faith and Practice in the Modern World*, ed. Mark A. Noll and David F. Wells (Grand Rapids, Mich.: Eerdmans, 1988), pp. 59-67.

[49]Tillard, "What Is the Church of God?" pp. 372-73.

[50]McDonnell, "Vatican II (1962-1964), Puebla (1979), Synod (1985)," p. 427.